falling
upward

RICHARD ROHR
falling
upward

a spirituality
for the two
halves of life

First published in Great Britain in 2012

Society for Promoting Christian Knowledge
36 Causton Street
London SW1P 4ST
www.spckpublishing.co.uk

Credits appear on page 199.

Readers should be aware that internet websites offered as citations and/or
sources for further information may have changed or disappeared
between the time this was written and when it is read.

SPCK does not necessarily endorse the individual views contained
in its publications.

British Library Cataloguing-in-Publication Data
A catalogue record for this book is available from the British Library

ISBN 978–0–281–06891–3

First printed in Great Britain by MPG Books
Subsequently digitally printed in Great Britain

Produced on paper from sustainable forests

CONTENTS

The Invitation to a Further Journey   vii
Introduction   xiii

1 The Two Halves of Life   1

2 The Hero and Heroine's Journey   17

3 The First Half of Life   25

4 The Tragic Sense of Life   53

5 Stumbling over the Stumbling Stone   65

6 Necessary Suffering   73

7 Home and Homesickness   87

8 Amnesia and the Big Picture   97

9 A Second Simplicity   105

10 A Bright Sadness   117

11 The Shadowlands   127

12 New Problems and New Directions   137

13 Falling Upward   153

Coda   161
Notes   169
Bibliography   177
The Author   183
Index   185

The greatest and most important problems of life are fundamentally unsolvable. They can never be solved, but only outgrown.
—CARL JUNG

 First there is the fall, and then we recover from the fall. Both are the mercy of God!
—LADY JULIAN OF NORWICH

To the Franciscan friars, my brothers, who trained me so well in the skills and spirituality of the first half of life that they also gave me the grounding, the space, the call, and the inevitability of a further and fantastic journey

A journey into the second half of our own lives awaits us all. Not everybody goes there, even though all of us get older, and some of us get older than others. A "further journey" is a well-kept secret, for some reason. Many people do not even know there is one. There are too few who are aware of it, tell us about it, or know that it is different from the journey of the first half of life. So why should I try to light up the path a little? Why should I presume that I have anything to say here? And why should I write to people who are still on their first journey, and happily so?

I am driven to write because after forty years as a Franciscan teacher, working in many settings, religions, countries, and institutions, I find that many, if not most, people and institutions remain stymied in the preoccupations of the first half of life. By that I mean that most people's concerns remain those of establishing their personal (or superior) identity, creating various boundary markers for themselves, seeking security, and perhaps linking to what seem like significant people or projects. These tasks are good to some degree and even necessary. We are all trying to find what the Greek philosopher Archimedes called a "lever and a place to stand" so that we can move the world just a little bit. The world would be much worse off if we did not do this first and important task.

But, in my opinion, this first-half-of-life task is no more than finding the starting gate. It is merely the warm-up act, not the full journey. It is the raft but not the shore. If you realize that there is a further journey, you might do the warm-up act quite differently, which would better prepare you for what follows. People at any age must know about the whole arc of their life and where it is tending and leading.

We know about this further journey from the clear and inviting voices of others who have been there, from the sacred and secular texts that invite us there, from our own observations of people who have entered this new territory, and also, sadly, from those who never seem to move on. The further journey usually appears like a seductive invitation and a kind of promise or hope. We are summoned to it, not commanded to go, perhaps because each of us has to go on this path freely, with all the messy and raw material of our own unique lives. But we don't have to do it, nor do we have to do it alone. There *are* guideposts, some common patterns, utterly new kinds of goals, a few warnings, and even personal guides on this further journey. I hope I can serve you in offering a bit of each of these in this book.

All of these sources and resources give me the courage and the desire to try to map the terrain of this further journey, along with the terrain of the first journey, but most especially the needed crossover points. As you will see from the chapter titles, I consider the usual crossover points to be a kind of "necessary suffering," stumbling over stumbling stones, and lots of shadowboxing, but often just a gnawing desire for "ourselves," for something more, or what I will call "homesickness."

I am trusting that you will see the truth of this map, yet it is the kind of soul truth that we only know "through a glass darkly" (1 Corinthians 13:12)—and through a glass brightly at the same time. Yet any glass through which we see is always made of human hands, like mine. All spiritual language is by necessity metaphor and symbol. The Light comes from elsewhere, yet it is necessarily reflected through those of us still walking on the journey ourselves. As Desmond Tutu told me on a recent trip to Cape Town, "We are only the light bulbs, Richard, and our job is just to remain screwed in!"

I believe that God gives us our soul, our deepest identity, our True Self,[1] our unique blueprint, at our own "immaculate conception." Our unique little bit of heaven is installed by the Manufacturer within the product, at the beginning! We are given a span of years to discover it, to choose it, and to live our own destiny to the full. If we do not, our True Self will never be offered again, in our own unique form—which is perhaps why almost all religious traditions present the matter with utterly charged words like "heaven" and "hell." Our soul's discovery is utterly crucial, momentous, and of pressing importance for each of us and for the world. We do not "make" or "create" our souls; we just "grow" them up. We are the clumsy stewards of our own souls. We are charged to awaken, and much of the work of spirituality is learning how to stay out of the way of this rather natural growing and awakening. We need to *unlearn* a lot, it seems, to get back to that foundational life which is "hidden in God" (Colossians 3:3). Yes, transformation is often more about unlearning than learning, which is why the religious traditions call it "conversion" or "repentance."

For me, no poet says this quite so perfectly as the literally *inimitable* Gerard Manley Hopkins in his Duns Scotus–inspired poem "As Kingfishers Catch Fire."[2]

Each mortal thing does one thing and the same:
Deals out that being indoors each one dwells;
Selves — goes itself; *myself* it speaks and spells,
Crying *what I do is me: for that I came.*

All we can give back and all God wants from any of us is to humbly and proudly return the product that we have been given — which is ourselves! If I am to believe the saints and mystics, this finished product is more valuable to God than it seemingly is to us. Whatever this Mystery is, we are definitely in on the deal! True religion is always a deep intuition that we are already *participating* in something very good, in spite of our best efforts to deny it or avoid it.

In fact, the best of modern theology is revealing a strong "turn toward participation," as opposed to religion as mere observation, affirmation, moralism, or group belonging. There is nothing to join, only something to recognize, suffer, and enjoy as a *participant*. You are already in the *eternal flow* that Christians would call the divine life of the Trinity.

Whether we find our True Self depends in large part on the moments of time we are each allotted, and the moments of freedom that we each receive and choose during that time. Life is indeed "momentous," created by accumulated moments in which the deeper "I" is slowly revealed if we are ready to see it. Holding our *inner blueprint*, which is a good description of our soul, and returning it humbly to the world and to God by love and service is indeed of ultimate concern. Each thing and every person must act out its nature fully, at whatever cost. It is our life's purpose, and the deepest meaning of "natural law." We are here to give back fully and freely what was first given to us — but now writ personally — by us! It is probably the most courageous and free act we will ever perform — and it takes both halves of our life to do it fully. The first half of life is discovering the script, and the second half is actually writing it and owning it.

So get ready for a great adventure, the one you were really born for. If we never get to our little bit of heaven, our life does not make much sense, and we have created our own "hell." So get ready for some new freedom, some dangerous permission, some hope from nowhere, some unexpected happiness, some stumbling stones, some radical grace, and some new and pressing responsibility for yourself and for our suffering world.

What is a normal goal to a young person becomes a neurotic hindrance in old age.
—CARL JUNG

 No wise person ever wanted to be younger.
—NATIVE AMERICAN APHORISM

There is much evidence on several levels that there are at least two major tasks to human life. The first task is to build a strong "container" or identity; the second is to find the contents that the container was meant to hold. The first task we take for granted as the very purpose of life, which does not mean we do it well. The second task, I am told, is more encountered than sought; few arrive at it with much preplanning, purpose, or passion. So you might wonder if there is much point in providing a guide to the territory ahead of time. Yet that is exactly why we must. It is vitally important to know what is coming and being offered to all of us.

We are a "first-half-of-life culture," largely concerned about *surviving successfully*. Probably most cultures and individuals across history have been situated in the first half of their own development up to now, because it is all they had time for. We all try to do what seems like the task that life first hands us: establishing an identity, a home, relationships, friends, community, security, and building a proper platform for our only life.

But it takes us much longer to discover "the task within the task," as I like to call it: *what we are really doing when we are doing what we are doing*. Two people can have the same job description, and one is holding a subtle or not-so-subtle life energy (*eros*) in doing his or her job, while another is holding a subtle or not-so-subtle negative energy (*thanatos*) while doing the exact same job. Most of us are somewhere in between, I suppose.

We actually respond to one another's energy more than to people's exact words or actions. In any situation, your taking or giving of energy is what you are actually doing. Everybody can feel, suffer, or enjoy the difference, but few can exactly say what it is that is happening. Why do I feel drawn or repelled? What we all desire and need from one another, of course, is that life energy called *eros*! It always draws, creates, and connects things.

This is surely what Jesus meant when he said that you could only tell a good tree from a bad one "by its fruits" (Matthew 7:20). Inside of life energy, a group or family will be productive and energetic; inside of death energy there will be gossip, cynicism, and mistrust hiding behind every interaction. Yet you usually cannot precisely put your finger on what is happening. That is second-half-of-life wisdom, or what Paul calls "the discerning of spirits" (1 Corinthians 12:10). Perhaps this book can be a school for such discernment and wisdom. That is surely my hope.

It is when we begin to pay attention, and seek integrity precisely in *the task within the task* that we begin to move from the first to the second half of our own lives. Integrity largely has to do with purifying our intentions and a growing honesty about our actual motives. It is hard work. Most often we don't pay attention to that inner task until we have had some kind of fall or failure in our outer tasks. This pattern is invariably true for reasons I have yet to fathom.

Life, if we are honest about it, is made up of many failings and fallings, amidst all of our hopeful growing and achieving. Those failings and fallings must be there for a purpose, a purpose that neither culture nor church has fully understood. Most of us find all failure bewildering, but it does not have to be. My observations tell me that if we can clarify the common *sequencing, staging,* and *direction of life's arc* a bit more, many practical questions and dilemmas will be resolved. That doesn't mean we can avoid the journey itself. Each of us still has to walk it for ourselves before we get the big picture of human life.

Maybe we should just call this book *Tips for the Road,* a sort of roadside assistance program. Or perhaps it is like a medical brochure that describes the possible symptoms of a future heart attack. Reading it when you're well might feel like a waste of time, but it could make the difference between life and death if a heart attack actually happens.

My assumption is that the second half of your own life *will* happen, although I hope it is not a heart attack (unless you understand "heart attack" symbolically, of course!).

When I say that you will enter the second half of life, I don't mean it in a strictly chronological way. Some young people, especially those who have learned from early suffering, are already there, and some older folks are still quite childish. If you are still in the first half of your life, chronologically or spiritually, I would hope that this book will offer you some good guidance, warnings, limits, permissions, and lots of possibilities. If you are in the second half of life already, I hope that this book will at least assure you that you are not crazy—and also give you some hearty bread for your whole journey.

None of us go into our spiritual maturity completely of our own accord, or by a totally free choice. We are led by *Mystery*, which religious people rightly call grace. Most of us have to be cajoled or seduced into it, or we fall into it by some kind of "transgression," believe it or not; like Jacob finding his birthright through cunning, and Esau losing his by failure (Genesis 27). Those who walk the full and entire journey are considered "called" or "chosen" in the Bible, perhaps "fated" or "destined" in world mythology and literature, but always they are the ones who have heard some deep invitation to "something more," and set out to find it by both grace and daring. Most get little reassurance from others, or even have full confidence that they are totally right. Setting out is always a leap of faith, a risk in the deepest sense of the term, and yet an adventure too.

The familiar and the habitual are so falsely reassuring, and most of us make our homes there permanently. The new is always by definition unfamiliar and untested, so God, life, destiny, suffering have to give us a push — usually a big one — or we will not go. Someone has to make clear to us that homes are not meant to be lived in — but only to be moved out from.

Most of us are never told that we can set out from the known and the familiar to take on a further journey. Our institutions and our expectations, including our churches, are almost entirely configured to encourage, support, reward, and validate the tasks of the first half of life. Shocking and disappointing, but I think it is true. We are more struggling to survive than to thrive, more just "getting through" or trying to get to the top than finding out what is really at the top or was already at the bottom. Thomas Merton, the American monk, pointed out that we may spend our whole life climbing the ladder of success, only to find when we get to the top that our ladder is leaning against the wrong wall.

Most of us in the first half of life suspect that all is not fully working, and we are probably right! It was not meant to stand alone. We were just told to build a nice basement and some kind of foundation for our house, but not given any plans or even a hint that we also needed to build an actual "living" room upstairs, let alone a nutritious kitchen or an erotic bedroom, and much less our own chapel. So many, if not most, of us settle for the brick and mortar of first-stage survival, and never get to what I will be calling "the unified field" of life itself. As Bill Plotkin, a wise guide, puts it, many of us learn to do our "survival dance," but we never get to our actual "sacred dance."

THE WAY UP AND THE WAY DOWN

The soul has many secrets. They are only revealed to those who want them, and are never completely forced upon us. One of the best-kept secrets, and yet one hidden in plain sight, is that *the way up is the way down*. Or, if you prefer, *the way down is the way up*. This pattern is obvious in all of nature, from the very change of seasons and substances on this earth, to the six hundred million tons of hydrogen that the sun burns every day to light and warm our earth, and even to the metabolic laws of dieting or fasting. The down-up pattern is constant, too, in mythology, in stories like that of Persephone, who must descend into the underworld and marry Hades for spring to be reborn.

In legends and literature, sacrifice of something to achieve something else is almost the only pattern. Dr. Faust has to sell his soul to the devil to achieve power and knowledge; Sleeping Beauty must sleep for a hundred years before she can receive the prince's kiss. In Scripture, we see that the wrestling and wounding of Jacob are necessary for Jacob to become Israel (Genesis 32:26–32), and the death and resurrection of Jesus are necessary to create Christianity. The loss and renewal pattern is so constant and ubiquitous that it should hardly be called a secret at all.

Yet it is still a secret, probably because we do not *want* to see it. We do not want to embark on a further journey if it feels like going down, especially after we have put so much sound and fury into going up. This is surely the first and primary reason why many people never get to the fullness of their own lives. The supposed achievements of the first half of life have to fall apart and show themselves to be wanting in some way, or we will not move further. Why would we?

Normally a job, fortune, or reputation has to be lost, a death has to be suffered, a house has to be flooded, or a disease has to be endured. The pattern in fact is so clear that one has to work rather hard, or be intellectually lazy, to miss the continual lesson. This, of course, was Scott Peck's major insight in his best-selling book, *The Road Less Traveled.* He told me personally once that he felt most Western people were just spiritually lazy. And when we are lazy, we stay on the path we are already on, even if it is going nowhere. It is the spiritual equivalent of the second law of thermodynamics: everything winds down unless some outside force winds it back up. True spirituality could be called the "outside force," although surprisingly it is found "inside," but we will get to that later.

Some kind of falling, what I will soon call "necessary suffering," is programmed into the journey. All the sources seem to say it, starting with Adam and Eve and all they represent. Yes, they "sinned" and were cast out of the Garden of Eden, but from those very acts came "consciousness," conscience, and their own further journey. But it all started with transgression. Only people unfamiliar with sacred story are surprised that they ate the apple. As soon as God told them specifically not to, you know they will! It creates the whole story line inside of which we can find ourselves.

It is not that suffering or failure *might* happen, or that it will only happen to you if you are bad (which is what religious people often think), or that it will happen to the unfortunate, or to a few in other places, or that you can somehow by cleverness or righteousness avoid it. No, it *will* happen, and to you! Losing, failing, falling, sin, and the suffering that comes from those experiences — all of this is a necessary and even good part of the human journey. As my favorite mystic, Lady Julian of Norwich, put it in her Middle English, "Sin is behovely!"

You cannot avoid sin or mistake anyway (Romans 5:12), but if you try too fervently, it often creates even worse problems. Jesus loves to tell stories like those of the publican and the Pharisee (Luke 18:9–14) and the famous one about the prodigal son (Luke 15:11–32), in which one character does his life totally right and is, in fact, wrong; and the other who does it totally wrong ends up God's beloved! Now deal with that! Jesus also tells us that there are two groups who are very good at trying to deny or avoid this humiliating surprise: *those who are very "rich" and those who are very "religious."* These two groups have very different plans for themselves, as they try to totally steer their own ships with well-chosen itineraries. They follow two different ways of going "up" and avoiding all "down."

Such a down-and-then-up perspective does not fit into our Western philosophy of progress, nor into our desire for upward mobility, nor into our religious notions of perfection or holiness. "Let's hope it is *not* true, at least for me," we all say! Yet the perennial tradition, sometimes called the wisdom tradition, says that it is and will always be true. St. Augustine called it the passing over mystery (or the "paschal mystery" from the Hebrew word for Passover, *pesach*).

Today we might use a variety of metaphors: reversing engines, a change in game plan, a falling off of the very wagon that we constructed. No one would choose such upheaval consciously; we must somehow "fall" into it. Those who are too carefully engineering their own superiority systems will usually not allow it at all. It is much more *done to you* than anything you do yourself, and sometimes nonreligious people are more open to this change in strategy than are religious folks who have their private salvation project all worked out. This is how I would interpret Jesus' enigmatic words, "The children of this world are wiser in their ways than the children of light" (Luke 16:8). I have met too many rigid and angry old Christians and clergy to deny this sad truth, but it seems to be true in all religions until and unless they lead to the actual transformation of persons.

In this book I would like to describe how this message of falling down and moving up is, in fact, the most counter-intuitive message in most of the world's religions, including and most especially Christianity. *We grow spiritually much more by doing it wrong than by doing it right*. That might just be the central message of how spiritual growth happens; yet nothing in us wants to believe it. I actually think it is the only workable meaning of any remaining notion of "original sin." There seems to have been a fly in the ointment from the beginning, but the key is recognizing and dealing with the fly rather than needing to throw out the whole ointment!

If there is such a thing as human perfection, it seems to emerge precisely from how we handle the imperfection that is everywhere, especially our own. What a clever place for God to hide holiness, so that only the humble and earnest will find it! A "perfect" person ends up being one who can consciously forgive and include imperfection rather than one who thinks he or she is totally above and beyond imperfection. It becomes sort of obvious once you say it out loud. In fact, I would say that *the demand for the perfect is the greatest enemy of the good*. Perfection is a mathematical or divine concept, goodness is a beautiful human concept that includes us all.

By denying their pain, avoiding the necessary falling, many have kept themselves from their own spiritual depths — and therefore have been kept from their own spiritual heights. First-half-of-life religion is almost always about various types of purity codes or "thou shalt nots" to keep us *up, clear, clean, and together*, like good Boy and Girl Scouts. A certain kind of "purity" and self-discipline is also "behovely," at least for a while in the first half of life, as the Jewish Torah brilliantly presents. I was a good Star Scout myself and a Catholic altar boy besides, who rode my bike to serve the 6 A.M. mass when I was merely ten years old. I hope you are as impressed as I was with myself.

Because none of us desire a downward path to growth through imperfection, seek it, or even suspect it, we have to get the message with the authority of a "divine revelation." So Jesus makes it into a central axiom: the "last" really do have a head start in moving toward "first," and those who spend too much time trying to be "first" will never get there. Jesus says this clearly in several places and in numerous parables, although those of us still on the first journey just cannot hear this. It has been considered mere religious fluff, as most of Western history has made rather clear. Our resistance to the message is so great that it could be called outright denial, even among sincere Christians. *The human ego prefers anything, just about anything, to falling or changing or dying*. The ego is that part of you that loves the status quo, even when it is not working. It attaches to past and present, and fears the future.

When you are in the first half of life, you cannot see any kind of failing or dying as even possible, much less as necessary or good. (Those who have *never* gone up, like the poor and the marginalized, may actually have a spiritual head start, according to Jesus!) But normally we need a few good successes to give us some ego structure and self-confidence, and to get us going. God mercifully hides thoughts of dying from the young, but unfortunately we then hide it from ourselves till the later years finally force it into our consciousness. Ernest Becker said some years ago that it is not love but "the denial of death" that might well make the world go round. What if he is right?

Some have called this principle of going down to go up a "spirituality of imperfection" or "the way of the wound." It has been affirmed in Christianity by St. Therese of Lisieux as her Little Way, by St. Francis as the way of poverty, and by Alcoholics Anonymous as the necessary first step. St. Paul taught this unwelcome message with his enigmatic "It is when I am weak that I am strong" (2 Corinthians 12:10). Of course, in saying that, he was merely building on what he called the "folly" of the crucifixion of Jesus—a tragic and absurd dying that became resurrection itself.

Like skaters, we move forward by actually moving from side to side. I found this phenomenon to be core and central in my research on male initiation,[1] and now we are finding it mirrored rather clearly in the whole universe, and especially in physics and biology, which is one huge pattern of entropy: constant loss and renewal, death and transformation, the changing of forms and forces. Some even see it in terms of "chaos theory": the exceptions are the only rule and then they create new rules. Scary, isn't it?

Denial of the pattern seems to be a kind of practical daily atheism or chosen ignorance among many believers and clergy. Many have opted for the soft religion of easy ego consolations, the human growth model, or the "prosperity Gospel" that has become so common in Western Christianity and in all the worlds we spiritually colonize. We do grow and increase, but by a far different path than the ego would ever imagine. Only the soul knows and understands.

What I hope to do in this small book, without a lot of need to convince anybody, is just to make *the sequencing, the tasks, and the direction* of the two halves of life clear. Then you will be ready to draw your own conclusions. That is why I have called it "falling upward." Those who are ready will see that this message is self-evident: those who have gone "down" are the only ones who understand "up." Those who have somehow fallen, and fallen well, are the only ones who can go up and not misuse "up." I want to describe what "up" in the second half of life will look like—and could look like! And, most especially, I want to explore how we transition from one to the other—*and how it is not by our own willpower or moral perfection.* It will be nothing like what we might have imagined beforehand, and we can't engineer it by ourselves. It is done unto us.

One more warning, if that is the right word: you will not know for sure that this message is true until you are on the "up" side. You will never imagine it to be true until you have gone through the "down" yourself and come out on the other side in larger form. You must be pressured "from on high," by fate, circumstance, love, or God, because nothing in you wants to believe it, or wants to go through it. Falling upward is a "secret" of the soul, known not by thinking about it or proving it but only by risking it—at least once. And by allowing yourself to be led—at least once. Those who have allowed it know it is true, but only after the fact.

This is probably why Jesus praised faith and trust even more than love. It takes a foundational trust to fall or to fail—and not to fall apart. Faith alone holds you while you stand waiting and hoping and trusting. Then, and only then, will deeper love happen. It's no surprise at all that in English (and I am told in other languages as well) we speak of "falling" in love. I think it is the only way to get there. None would go freely, if we knew ahead of time what love is going to ask of us. Very human faith lays the utterly needed foundation for the ongoing discovery of love. Have no doubt, though: *great love is always a discovery, a revelation, a wonderful surprise, a falling into "something" much bigger and deeper that is literally beyond us and larger than us.*

Jesus tells the disciples as they descend from the mountain of transfiguration, "Do not talk about these things until the Human One is risen from the dead" (by which he means until you are on the other side of loss and renewal). If you try to assert wisdom before people have themselves walked it, be prepared for much resistance, denial, push-back, and verbal debate. As the text in Mark continues, "the disciples continued to discuss among themselves what 'rising from the dead' might even mean" (Mark 9:9–10). You cannot imagine a new space fully until you have been taken there. I make this point strongly to help you understand why almost all spiritual teachers tell you to "believe" or "trust" or "hold on." *They are not just telling you to believe silly or irrational things.* They are telling you to hold on until you can go on the further journey for yourself, and they are telling you that the whole spiritual journey is, in fact, for real—which you cannot possibly know yet.

The language of the first half of life and the language of the second half of life are almost two different vocabularies, known only to those who have been in both of them. The advantage of those on the further journey is that they can still remember and respect the first language and task. *They have transcended but also included all that went before.* In fact, if you cannot include and integrate the wisdom of the first half of life, I doubt if you have moved to the second. Never throw out the baby with the bathwater. People who know how to creatively break the rules also know why the rules were there in the first place. They are not mere iconoclasts or rebels.

I have often thought that this is the symbolic meaning of Moses breaking the first tablets of the law, only to go back up the mountain and have them redone (Exodus 32:19–34, 35) by Yahweh. The second set of tablets emerges after a face-to-face encounter with God, which changes everything. Our first understanding of law must fail us and disappoint us. Only after breaking the first tablets of the law is Moses a real leader and prophet. Only afterwards does he see God's glory (Exodus 33:18f), and only afterwards does his face "shine" (Exodus 34:29f). It might just be the difference between the two halves of life!

The Dalai Lama said much the same thing: "Learn and obey the rules very well, so you will know how to break them properly." Such discrimination between means and goals is almost the litmus test of whether you are moving in the right direction, and all the world religions at the mature levels will say similar things. For some reason, religious people tend to confuse the means with the actual goal. In the beginning, you tend to think that God really cares about your exact posture, the exact day of the week for public prayer, the authorship and wordings of your prayers, and other such things. Once your life has become a constant communion, you know that all the techniques, formulas, sacraments, and practices were just a dress rehearsal for the real thing—life itself—which can actually become a constant intentional prayer. Your conscious and loving existence gives glory to God.

All of this talk of the first and second half of life, of the languages of each, of falling down to go up is not new. It has been embodied for centuries in mythic tales of men and women who found themselves on the further journey. We will now take a closer look at one of the most famous.

A FOUNDING MYTH

Western rationalism no longer understands myths, and their importance, although almost all historic cultures did.[2] We are the obvious exception, and have replaced these effective and healing story lines with ineffective, cruel, and disorienting narratives like communism, fascism, terrorism, mass production, and its counterpart, consumerism. In other words, we all have our de facto worldviews that determine what is important and what is not important to us. They usually have a symbolic story to hold them together, such as that of "Honest Abe" chopping wood in Kentucky and educating himself in Illinois. "Myths" like this become a standing and effective metaphor for the American worldview of self-determination, hard work, and achievement. Whether they are exact historical truth is not even important.

Such myths proceed from the deep and collective unconscious of humanity. Our myths are stories or images that are not always true in particular but entirely true in general. They are usually not historical fact, but invariably they are spiritual genius. They hold life and death, the explainable and the unexplainable together as one; they hold together the paradoxes that the rational mind cannot process by itself. As good poetry does, myths make unclear and confused emotions brilliantly clear and life changing.

Myths are true basically because they work! A sacred myth keeps a people healthy, happy, and whole — even inside their pain. They give deep meaning, and pull us into "deep time" (which encompasses all time, past and future, geological and cosmological, and not just our little time or culture). Such stories are the very food of the soul, and they are what we are trying to get back to when we start fairy tales with phrases like "Once upon a time" or "Long ago, in a faraway land." Catholics used to say at the end of their Latin prayers, *Per omnia saecula saeculorum*, loosely translated as "through all the ages of ages." Somehow deep time orients the psyche, gives ultimate perspective, realigns us, grounds us, and thus heals us. We belong to a Mystery far grander than our little selves and our little time. Great storytellers and spiritual teachers always know this.

Remember, the opposite of rational is not always irrational, but it can also be *transrational* or bigger than the rational mind can process; things like love, death, suffering, God, and infinity are transrational experiences. Both myth and mature religion understand this. The transrational has the capacity to keep us inside an open system and a larger horizon so that the soul, the heart, and the mind do not close down inside of small and constricted space. The merely rational mind is invariably dualistic, and divides the field of almost every moment between what it can presently understand and what it then deems "wrong" or untrue.[3] Because the rational mind cannot process love or suffering, for example, it tends to either avoid them, deny them, or blame somebody for them, when in fact they are the greatest spiritual teachers of all, if we but allow them. Our loss of mythic consciousness has not served the last few centuries well, and has overseen the growth of rigid fundamentalism in all the world religions. Now we get trapped in destructive and "invisible" myths because we do not have the eyes to see how great healing myths function.

The Odyssey

The story of Odysseus is a classic transrational myth, one that many would say sets the bar and direction for all later Western storytelling. We all have our own little "odysseys," but the word came from the name of one man, who fought, sailed, and lived a classic pattern of human, tragic, and heroic life many centuries ago.

In Homer's tale *The Odyssey,* written around 700 B.C., we follow the awesome and adventurous journey of the hero Odysseus as he journeys home from the Trojan war. Rowing his boat past seductive sirens, with detours because of the one-eyed cyclops and the lotus eaters, on through the straits of Scylla and Charybdis, through the consolations and confusions of both Circe and Calypso, Odysseus tries to get back home. Through trial, guile, error, and ecstasy, chased by gods and monsters, Odysseus finally returns home to his island, Ithaca, to reunion with his beloved wife, Penelope; his old, dear father, Laertes; his longing son, Telemachus; and even his dying dog, Argos. Great and good stuff!

Accustomed as we are to our normal story line, we rightly expect a "happily ever after" ending to Odysseus's tale. And for most readers, that is all, in fact, they need, want, or remember from the story. Odysseus did return, reclaim his home, and reunite with his wife, son, and father. But there is more! In the final two chapters, after what seems like a glorious and appropriate ending, Homer announces and calls Odysseus to *a new and second journey* that is barely talked about, yet somehow Homer deemed it absolutely necessary to his character's life.

Instead of settling into quiet later years, Odysseus knows that he must heed the prophecy he has already received, *but half forgotten*, from the blind seer Teiresias and leave home once again. It is his fate, required by the gods. This new journey has no detailed description, only a few very telling images. I wonder, in 700 B.C., before we began to fully understand and speak about the second-half-of-life journey, whether Homer simply intuited that there had to be *something more*, as Greek literature often did.

> *Then came also the ghost of Theban Teiresias, with his golden sceptre in his hand. . . . When you get home you will take your revenge on these suitors of your wife; and after you have killed them by force or fraud in your own house, you must take a well-made oar and carry it on and on, till you come to a country where the people have never heard of the sea and do not even mix salt with their food, nor do they know anything about ships, and oars that are as the wings of a ship. I will give you this certain token which cannot escape your notice. A wayfarer will meet you and will say [your oar] must be a winnowing shovel that you have got upon your shoulder; on [hearing] this you must fix the oar in the ground and sacrifice a ram, a bull, and a boar to Neptune. Then go home and offer hecatombs [one hundred cattle] to the gods in heaven one after the other. As for yourself, death shall come to you from the sea, and your life shall ebb away very gently when you are full of years and peace of mind, and your people shall bless you. All that I have said will come true.*[4]

Teiresias's prophecy, which Odysseus half heard earlier in the story, seems to be an omen of what will happen to all of us. Here is my summary of the key points for our purposes, which I hope you will find very telling:

1.   Odysseus receives this prophecy at the point in his story when he is traveling through Hades, the kingdom of the dead and thus "at the bottom," as it were. It is often when the ego is most deconstructed that we can hear things anew and begin some honest reconstruction, even if it is only half heard and halfhearted.

2.   Teiresias is "holding a golden sceptre" when he gives Odysseus the message. I would interpret that as a symbol of the message's coming from a divine source, an authority from without and beyond, unsolicited or unsought, and maybe even unwanted by Odysseus himself. Often it takes outer authority to send us on the path toward our own inner authority.

3.   After all his attempts to return there, Odysseus is fated again to leave Ithaca, which is an island, and go to the "mainland" for a further journey; he is reuniting his small "island part" with the big picture, as it were. For me, this is what makes something inherently religious: whatever reconnects (*re-ligio*) our parts to the Whole is an experience of God, whether we call it that or not. He is also reconnecting his outer journey to the "inland" or his

interior world, which is much of the task of the second half of life. What brilliant metaphors!

4. He is to carry the oar, which was his "delivery system" as one who journeyed by ship in his first life. But a wayfarer he meets far from the ocean will see it instead as a winnowing shovel, a tool for separating grain from chaff! When he meets this wayfarer, this is the sign that he has reached the end of his further journey, and he is to plant the oar in the ground at that spot and leave it there (much as young men bury their childhood toys at a male initiation rite today) and only then can he finally return home. The first world of occupation and productivity must now find its full purpose.

5. Then he is to sacrifice to the god Neptune, who has been on his trail throughout the first journey. The language of offering sacrifice is rather universal in ancient myths. It must have been recognized that to go forward there is always something that has to be let go of, moved beyond, given up, or "forgiven" to enter the larger picture of the "gods."

6. He is to sacrifice three specific things: a wild bull, a breeding boar, and a battering ram. I doubt whether we could come up with three more graphic images of untrained or immature male energy. (Women will want to find their own counterparts here.) You cannot walk the second journey with first journey tools. You need a whole new tool kit.

7.   After this further journey, he is to return home to Ithaca, "to prepare a solemn sacrifice to all the gods who rule the broad heavens." In human language, he is finally living inside the big and true picture; in Christian language, he is finally connected to the larger "Kingdom of God."

8.   Only after this further journey and its sacrifices can Odysseus say that he will "live happily with my people around me, until I sink under the comfortable burden of years, and death will come to me gently from the sea." Death is largely a threat to those who have not yet lived their life. Odysseus has lived the journeys of both halves of life, and is ready to freely and finally let go.

Talk about the wisdom of the deep unconscious! God did not need to wait until we organized human spiritual intuitions into formal religions. The Spirit has been hovering over our chaos since the beginning, according to the second verse of the Bible (Genesis 1:2), and over all creation since the beginning of time (Romans 1:20). Homer was not just a "pagan" Greek, and we are not necessarily wiser because we live twenty-seven hundred years later.

Now put this powerful myth in the back of your mind as we dive into this exciting exploration of the further journey. It can operate as a sort of blueprint for what we want to say. Just remember this much consciously: *the whole story is set in the matrix of seeking to find home and then to return there, and thus refining and defining what home really is.*

Home is both the beginning and the end. Home is not a sentimental concept at all, but an inner compass and a North Star at the same time. It is a metaphor for the soul.

And yes, my female readers, it is an old male story and reflects issues from that side of the gender divide. But it is true for you too, in ways that you will discover.

THE TWO HALVES OF LIFE

 One cannot live the afternoon of life according to the program of life's morning; for what was great in the morning will be of little importance in the evening, and what in the morning was true will at evening have become a lie.

—CARL JUNG, *THE STRUCTURE AND DYNAMICS OF THE PSYCHE*

As I began to say in the Introduction, the task of the first half of life is to create a proper *container* for one's life and answer the first essential questions: "What makes me significant?" "How can I support myself?" and "Who will go with me?" The task of the second half of life is, quite simply, to find the actual *contents* that this container was meant to hold and deliver. As Mary Oliver puts it, "What is it you plan to do with your one wild and precious life?" In other words, the container is not an end in itself, but exists for the sake of your deeper and fullest life, which you largely do not know about yourself! Far too many people just keep doing repair work on the container itself and never "throw their nets into the deep" (John 21:6) to bring in the huge catch that awaits them.

Problematically, the first task invests so much of our blood, sweat, eggs and sperm, tears and years that we often cannot imagine there is a second task, or that anything more could be expected of us. "The old wineskins are good enough" (Luke 5:39), we say, even though according to Jesus they often cannot hold the new wine. According to him, if we do not get some new wineskins, "the wine and the wineskin will both be lost." The second half of life can hold some new wine because by then there should be some strong wineskins, some tested ways of holding our lives together. But that normally means that the container itself has to stretch, die in its present form, or even replace itself with something better. This is the big rub, as they say, but also the very source of our midlife excitement and discovery.

Various traditions have used many metaphors to make this differentiation clear: beginners and proficients, novices and initiated, milk and meat, letter and spirit, juniors and seniors, baptized and confirmed, apprentice and master, morning and evening, "Peter when you were young . . . Peter when you are old" (John 21:18). Only when you have begun to live in the second half can you see the difference between the two. Yet the two halves are *cumulative and sequential, and both are very necessary*. You cannot do a nonstop flight to the second half of life by reading lots of books about it, including this one. Grace must and will edge you forward. "God has no grandchildren. God only has children," as some have said. Each generation has to make its own discoveries of Spirit for itself. If not, we just react to the previous generation, and often overreact. Or we conform, and often overconform. Neither is a positive or creative way to move forward.

No Pope, Bible quote, psychological technique, religious formula, book, or guru can do your journey for you. If you try to skip the first journey, you will never see its real necessity and also its limitations; you will never know why this first container *must* fail you, the wonderful fullness of the second half of the journey, and the relationship between the two. Such is the unreality of many people who "never grow up" or who remain narcissistic into their old age. I am afraid this is not a small number of people in our world today.

"Juniors" on the first part of the journey invariably think that true elders are naive, simplistic, "out of it," or just superfluous. They cannot understand what they have not yet experienced. They are totally involved in their first task, and cannot see beyond it. Conversely, if a person has transcended and included the previous stages, he or she will always have a patient understanding of the juniors, and can be patient and helpful to them somewhat naturally (although not without trial and effort). That is precisely what makes such people elders! *Higher stages always empathetically include the lower, or they are not higher stages!*

Almost all of culture, and even most of religious history, has been invested in the creation and maintenance of first-half-of-life issues: the big three concerns of identity, security, and sexuality and gender. They don't just preoccupy us; they totally take over. That is where history has been up to now, I am afraid. In fact, most generations have seen boundary marking and protecting those boundaries as their primary and sometimes only task in life. Most of history has been the forging of structures of security and appropriate loyalty symbols, to announce and defend one's personal identity, one's group, and one's gender issues and identity. Now we seem to live in a time when more and more people are asking, "Is that all there is?"

In our formative years, we are so self-preoccupied that we are both overly defensive and overly offensive at the same time, with little time left for simply living, pure friendship, useless beauty, or moments of communion with nature or anything. Yet that kind of ego structuring is exactly what a young person partly needs to get through the first twenty years or so, and what tribes need to survive. Maybe it is what humanity needed to get started. "Good fences make good neighbors," Robert Frost said, but he also presumed that you don't just build fences. You eventually need to cross beyond them too, to actually meet the neighbor.

So we need boundaries, identity, safety, and some degree of order and consistency to get started personally and culturally. We also need to feel "special"; we need our "narcissistic fix." By that I mean, we all need some successes, response, and positive feedback early in life, or we will spend the rest of our lives demanding it, or bemoaning its lack, from others. There is a good and needed "narcissism," if you want to call it that. You have to first have an ego structure to then let go of it and move beyond it. Responding to John the Baptist's hard-line approach, Jesus maintains both sides of this equation when he says, "No man born of woman is greater than John the Baptizer, yet the least who enters the kingdom of heaven is greater than he is" (Matthew 11:11). Is that double-talk? No, it is second-half-of-life talk.

Basically if you get mirrored well early in life, you do not have to spend the rest of your life looking in Narcissus's mirror or begging for the attention of others. You have already been "attended to," and now feel basically good—and always will. If you were properly mirrored when you were young, you are now free to mirror others and see yourself—honestly and helpfully. I can see why a number of saints spoke of prayer itself as simply receiving the ever-benevolent gaze of God, returning it in kind, mutually gazing, and finally recognizing that it is one single gaze received and bounced back. The Hindus called this exciting mutual beholding *darshan*. We will talk more about this mirroring toward the end of the book.

Once you have your narcissistic fix, you have no real need to protect your identity, defend it, prove it, or assert it. It just is, and is more than enough. This is what we actually mean by "salvation," especially when we get our narcissistic fix all the way from the Top. When you get your "Who am I?" question right, all the "What should I do?" questions tend to take care of themselves. The very fact that so many religious people have to so vigorously prove and defend their salvation theories makes one seriously doubt whether they have experienced divine mirroring at any great depth.

In the first half of life, success, security, and containment—"looking good" to ourselves and others— are almost the only questions. They are the early stages in Maslow's "hierarchy of needs."[1] In a culture like ours, still preoccupied with security issues, enormously high military budgets are never seriously questioned by Congress or by the people, while appropriations reflecting later stages in the hierarchy of needs, like those for education, health care for the poor, and the arts, are quickly cut, if even considered. The message is clear that we are largely an adolescent culture. Religions, similarly, *need* to make truth claims that are absolutely absolute—and we want them for just that—because they are absolute! This feels right and necessary at this early stage, despite any talk of Biblical "faith" or trust, which can only be comprehended later.

We all want and need various certitudes, constants, and insurance policies at every stage of life. *But we have to be careful, or they totally take over and become all-controlling needs, keeping us from further growth.* Thus the most common one-liner in the Bible is "Do not be afraid"; in fact, someone counted and found that it occurs 365 times! If we do not move beyond our early motivations of personal security, reproduction, and survival (the fear-based preoccupations of the "lizard brain"), we will never proceed beyond the lower stages of human or spiritual development. Many church sermons I have heard my whole life seem never to move beyond this first level of development, and do not even challenge it. In fact, to challenge it is called heretical, dangerous, or ill advised.

The very unfortunate result of this preoccupation with order, control, safety, pleasure, and certitude is that a high percentage of people never get to the contents of their own lives! Human life is about more than building boundaries, protecting identities, creating tribes, and teaching impulse control. As Jesus said, "Why do you ask, what am I to eat? What am I to wear?" And to that he says, "Is life not so much more than food? Is life not so much more than clothing?" (Luke 12:23). "What will it profit you if you gain the whole world, and lose your very soul?" (Matthew 16:26).

There is too much defensive behavior and therefore too much offensive behavior in the first half of life to get to the really substantial questions, which are what drive you forward on the further journey. Human maturity is neither offensive nor defensive; it is finally able to accept that reality *is what it is*. Ken Keyes so wisely said, "More suffering comes into the world by people taking offense than by people intending to give offense." The offended ones feel the need to offend back those who they think have offended them, creating defensiveness on the part of the presumed offenders, which often becomes a new offensive—ad infinitum. There seems to be no way out of this self-defeating and violent Ping-Pong game—except growing up spiritually. The True Self, you see, is very hard to offend!

STEPS AND STAGES

It was Carl Jung who first popularized the phrase "the two halves of life" to describe these two major tangents and tasks, yet many other teachers have recognized that there are clear stages and steps of human and spiritual maturation. Process language is not new; it has just used different images.

There is the foundational journey of Abraham and Sarah; the Exodus of Moses; Mohammed's several key flights; Jesus' four kinds of soil; the "way of the cross" images on the walls of churches; John of the Ladder; the recurring schemas of Sts. Bonaventure, John of the Cross, and Teresa of Avila; and in the modern era, Jean Piaget, James Fowler, Lawrence Kohlberg, Clare Graves, Jean Gebser, Abraham Maslow, Erik Erikson, Ken Wilber, Carol Gilligan, Daniel Levinson, Bill Plotkin, and the entire world of "Spiral Dynamics." They all affirm that growth and development have a direction and are not a static "grit your teeth and bear it." *Unless you can chart and encourage both movement and direction, you have no way to name maturity or immaturity*. Most of these teachers, each in his or her own way, seem to coalesce around two key insights that continue to show themselves in almost every one of these constructs.

First of all, you can only see and understand the earlier stages from the wider perspective of the later stages. This is why mature societies were meant to be led by elders, seniors, saints, and "the initiated." They alone are in a position to be true leaders in a society, or certainly in any spiritual organization. Without them, "the blind lead the blind," which is typified by phenomena like violent gangs of youth or suicide bombers. Those who are not true leaders or elders will just affirm people at their own immature level, and of course immature people will love them and elect them for being equally immature. You can fill in the names here with your own political disaster story. But just remember, there is a symbiosis between immature groups and immature leaders, I am afraid, which is why both Plato and Jefferson said democracy was not really the best form of government. It is just the safest. A truly wise monarch would probably be the most effective at getting things done. (Don't send hate letters, please!)

If you have, in fact, deepened and grown "in wisdom, age, and grace" (Luke 2:52), you are able to be patient, inclusive, and understanding of all the previous stages. That is what I mean by my frequent use of the phrase "transcend and include." That is the infallible sign that you are enlightened, psychologically mature, or a truly adult believer. The "adepts" in all religions are always forgiving, compassionate, and radically inclusive. They do not create enemies, and they move beyond the boundaries of their own "starter group" while still honoring them and making use of them. Jesus the Jew criticizes his own religion the most, yet never leaves it! Mature people are not either-or thinkers, but they bathe in the ocean of both-and. (Think Gandhi, Anne Frank, Martin Luther King Jr., Mother Teresa, Nelson Mandela, and the like.) These enlightened people tend to grease the wheels of religious evolution. As Albert Einstein said, "No problem can be solved by the same consciousness that caused it in the first place." God moves humanity and religion forward by the regular appearance of such whole and holy people.

The second insight about steps and stages is that from your own level of development, you can only stretch yourself to comprehend people just a bit beyond yourself. Some theorists say you cannot stretch more than one step above your own level of consciousness, and that is on a good day! Because of this limitation, those at deeper (or "higher") levels beyond you invariably appear wrong, sinful, heretical, dangerous, or even worthy of elimination. How else can we explain the consistent killing of prophets; the marginalization of truly holy people as naive; the rather consistent racism, self-protectiveness, and warlike attitudes of people who think of themselves as civilized? You can be "civilized" and still be judging from the fully egocentric position of an early level of development. In fact, one of the best covers for very narcissistic people is to be polite, smiling, and thoroughly civilized. Hitler loved animals and classical music, I am told.

If change and growth are not *programmed into* your spirituality, if there are not serious warnings about the blinding nature of fear and fanaticism, your religion will *always* end up worshiping the status quo and protecting your present ego position and personal advantage — as if it were God! Although Jesus' first preached message is clearly "change!" (as in Mark 1:15 and Matthew 4:17), where he told his listeners to "repent," which literally means to "change your mind," it did not strongly influence Christian history. This resistance to change is so common, in fact, that it is almost what we expect from religious people, who tend to love the past more than the future or the present. All we can conclude is that much of organized religion is itself living inside of first-half-of-life issues, which usually coincides with where most people are in any culture. We all receive and pass on what our people are prepared to hear, and most people are not "early adopters." Yet even the intelligence of animals is determined by their ability to change and adjust their behavior in response to new circumstances. Those who do not, become extinct.

This pattern of resistance is so clear and even so defeating for Jesus that he makes what sounds like one of his most unkind statements: "Do not give to dogs what is holy, or throw your pearls before swine. They will trample them, and then they will turn on you and tear you to pieces" (Matthew 7:6). We can save ourselves a lot of distress and accusation by knowing when, where, to whom, and how to talk about spiritually mature things. We had best offer what each one is ready to hear, and perhaps only stretching them a bit! Ken Wilber says that most of us are only willing to call 5 percent of our present information into question at any one point—and again that is on a very good day. I guess prophets are those who do not care whether you are ready to hear their message. They say it because it has to be said and because it is true.

If there is no wise authority capable of protecting them and validating them, most prophetic or wise people and all "early adopters" are almost always "torn to pieces." Their wisdom sounds like dangerous foolishness, like most of Jesus' Sermon on the Mount to Christians, like Gandhi to Great Britain, like Martin Luther King Jr. to white America, like Nelson Mandela to Dutch Reformed South Africa, like Harriet Tubman to the Daughters of the American Revolution, like American nuns to the Catholic patriarchy.

OF GOD AND RELIGION

Theologically and objectively speaking, we are already in union with God. But it is very hard for people to believe or experience this when they have no positive sense of identity, little courage yet, no strong boundaries to contain Mystery, and little inner religious experience at any depth. Thus the first journey is always about externals, formulas, superficial emotions, flags and badges, correct rituals, Bible quotes, and special clothing, all of which largely substitute for actual spirituality (see Matthew 23:13–32). Yet they are all used and needed to create the container. Yes, it is largely style and sentiment instead of real substance, but even that is probably necessary. Just don't give your life for mere style and sentiment. Pope John XXIII's motto might be heard here: "In essentials unity, in nonessentials liberty, and in all things, charity." That is second-half-of-life, hard-won wisdom.

In the first half of our lives, we have no container for such awesome content, no wineskins that are prepared to hold such utterly intoxicating wine. You see, *authentic God experience always "burns" you, yet does not destroy you* (Exodus 3:2–3), just as the burning bush did to Moses. But most of us are not prepared for such burning, nor even told to expect it. The Islamic mystics seem to be the most honest here, as we see in the ecstatic and erotic poetry of Rumi, Kabir, and Hafiz. By definition, authentic God experience is always "too much"! It consoles our True Self only after it has devastated our false self. We must begin to be honest about this instead of dishing out fast-food religion.[2]

Early-stage religion is largely preparing you for the immense gift of this burning, this inner experience of God, as though creating a proper stable into which the Christ can be born. Unfortunately, most people get so preoccupied with their stable, and whether their stable is better than your stable, or whether their stable is the only "one, holy, catholic, and apostolic" stable, that they never get to the birth of God in the soul. There is no indication in the text that Jesus demanded ideal stable conditions; in fact, you could say that the specific mentioning of his birth in a "manger" is making the exact opposite point. Animals at least had room for him, while there was "no room for him in the inn" (Luke 2:8) where humans dwelled.

As a priest of forty years, I find that much of the spiritual and pastoral work of churches is often ineffective at the levels of real transformation, and calls forth immense passivity and even many passive-aggressive responses. As a preacher, I find that I am forced to dumb down the material in order to interest a Sunday crowd that does not expect or even want any real challenge; nor does it exhibit much spiritual or intellectual curiosity. "Just repeat what I expect to hear, Father, and maybe a joke or two!" As a spiritual director, I find that most people facing the important transformative issues of social injustice, divorce, failure, gender identity, an inner life of prayer, or any radical reading of the Gospel are usually bored and limited by the typical Sunday church agenda. And these are good people! But they keep on doing their own kind of survival dance, because no one has told them about their sacred dance. Of course, clergy cannot talk about a further journey if they have not gone on it themselves.

In short, we have not found a way to do the age-appropriate tasks of the two halves of life, and both groups are losing out. The juniors are made to think that the container is all there is and all they should expect; or worse, that they are mature and home free because they believe a few right things or perform some right rituals. The would-be maturing believer is not challenged to any adult faith or service to the world, much less mystical union. Everyone ends up in a muddled middle, where "the best lack all conviction, while the worst are full of passionate intensity," as William Butler Yeats put it. I am convinced that much of this pastoral and practical confusion has emerged because we have not clarified the real differences, the needs, and the somewhat conflicting challenges of the two halves of our own lives. So let's try.

CHAPTER 2

THE HERO AND HEROINE'S JOURNEY

 We have only to follow the thread of the hero path. Where we had thought to find an abomination, we shall find a god; where we had thought to slay another, we shall slay ourselves; where we had thought to travel outwards, we shall come to the center of our own existence; where we had thought to be alone, we shall be with all the world.

—JOSEPH CAMPBELL, *THE HERO WITH A THOUSAND FACES*

If you look at the world's mythologies in any of the modern collections, you will invariably see what Joseph Campbell calls the "monomyth of the hero" repeated in various forms for both men and women, but with different symbols.[1] The stages of the hero's journey are a skeleton of what this book wants to say! In some ways, we are merely going to unpack this classic journey and draw out many of the implications that are even clearer today, both psychologically and spiritually. We are the beneficiaries of spiritual and informational globalization, like no one has ever been before.

17

The pattern of the heroic journey is rather consistent and really matches my own research on initiation.[2] Those embarking on this journey invariably go through the following stages in one form or another.

1.   They live in a world that they presently take as given and sufficient; they are often a prince or princess and, if not, sometimes even of divine origin, which of course they always know nothing about! (This amnesia is a giveaway for the core religious problem, as discovering our divine DNA is always the task.) Remember, Odysseus is the king of Ithaca, but does not "reign" there until after the second journey.

2.   They have the call or the courage to leave home for an adventure of some type—not really to solve any problem, but just to *go out and beyond their present comfort zone*. For example, the young Siddhartha leaves the walls of the palace, St. Francis goes on pilgrimages to the Muslim world, Queen Esther and Joan of Arc enter the world of battle to protect their peoples, Odysseus sets out for the Trojan war.

3.   On this journey or adventure, they in fact *find their real problem*! They are almost always "wounded" in some way and encounter a major dilemma, and the whole story largely pivots around the resolution of the trials that result. There is *always* a wounding; and the great epiphany is that the wound becomes the secret key, even "sacred," a wound

that changes them dramatically, which, by the way, is the precise meaning of the wounds of Jesus!

Their world is opened up, the screen becomes much larger, and they do too. Our very word *odyssey* is now used to describe these kinds of discoveries and adventures. Odysseus enters the story as a man alone weeping on a beach, defeated, with no hope of ever returning home, where he would be a hero. That is his gnawing and unending wound. It is all so unfair, because he was a hero in the Trojan war.

4.   The first task, which the hero or heroine thinks is the only task, is only the vehicle and warm-up act to get him or her to the real task. He or she "falls through" what is merely *his or her life situation* to discover his or her *Real Life*, which is always a much deeper river, hidden beneath the appearances. Most people confuse their life situation with their actual life, which is an underlying flow beneath the everyday events. This deeper discovery is largely what religious people mean by "finding their soul."

5.   The hero or heroine then returns to where he or she started, and "knows the place for the first time," as T. S. Eliot puts it; but now with a gift or "boon" for his people or her village. As the last step of Alcoholics Anonymous says, a person must *pass the lessons learned on to others — or there has been no real gift at all.* The hero's journey is always an experience of an excess of life, a surplus of energy, with plenty left over for others. The hero or heroine has found

eros or life energy, and it is more than enough to undo *thanatos,* the energy of death.

If it is authentic life energy, it is always experienced as a surplus or an abundance of life. The hero or heroine is by definition a "generative" person, to use Erik Erikson's fine term, concerned about the next generation and not just himself or herself. The hero lives in deep time and not just in his or her own small time. In fact, I would wonder if you could be a hero or heroine if you did not live in what many call deep time—that is, past, present, and future all at once.

———

Interestingly enough, this classic tradition of a true "hero" is not our present understanding at all. There is little social matrix to our present use of the word. A "hero" now is largely about being bold, muscular, rich, famous, talented, or "fantastic" by himself, and often *for* himself, whereas the classic hero is one who "goes the distance," whatever that takes, and then has plenty left over for others. True heroism serves the common good, or it is not really heroism at all.

To seek one's own *American Idol* fame, power, salary, or talent might historically have made one famous, or even infamous—but not a hero or heroine. To be a celebrity or a mere survivor today is often confused with heroism, probably a sign of our actual regression. Merely to survive and preserve our life is a low-level instinct that we share with good little lizards, but it is not heroism in any classic sense. We were meant to thrive and not just survive. We are glad when someone survives, and that surely took some courage and effort. But what are you going to do with your now resurrected life? That is the heroic question.

The very first sign of a potential hero's journey is that he or she must leave home, the familiar, which is something that may not always occur to someone in the first half of life. (In fact, many people have not left home by their thirties today, and most never leave the familiar at all!) If you have spent many years building your particular tower of success and self-importance — your personal "salvation project," as Thomas Merton called it — or have successfully constructed your own superior ethnic group, religion, or "house," you won't want to leave it. (Now that many people have second, third, and fourth houses, it makes me wonder how they can ever leave home.)

Once you can get "out of the house," your "castle" and comfort zone, much of the journey has a life — and death — of its own. The crucial thing is to get out and about, and into the real and bigger issues. In fact, this was the basic plotline of the founding myth that created the three monotheistic religions, with Yahweh's words to Abraham and Sarah: "Leave your country, your family, and your father's house, for the new land that I will show you"

(Genesis 12:1). We seem to have an amazing capacity for missing the major point—and our own necessary starting point along with it. We have rather totally turned around our very founding myth! No wonder religion is in trouble.

I wonder whether we no longer have that real "obedience to the gods," or sense of destiny, call, and fate that led Odysseus to leave father, wife, and son for a second journey. That is the very same obedience, by the way, that Jesus scandalously talks about in several places like Luke 14:26 ("If any one comes to me without leaving his own father and mother and wife and children and brothers and sisters, yes, and even his own life, he cannot be my disciple"). I always wonder what so-called family values Christians do with shocking lines like that? Jesus was not a nuclear family man at all, by any common definition! What led so many saints to seek the "will of God" first and above their own? What has led so many Peace Corps workers, missionaries, and skilled people to leave their countries for difficult lands and challenges? I would assume it was often a sense of a further journey, an invitation from their soul, or even a deep obedience to God.

Most of the calls of the disciples in the New Testament are rather clearly invitations to leave "your father and your nets" (Matthew 4:22). When he calls his first disciples, Jesus is talking about further journeys to people who are already happily settled and religiously settled! He is not talking about joining a new security system or a religious denomination or even a religious order that pays all your bills. Again, it is very surprising to me that so many Christians who read the Scriptures do not see this. Yet maybe they cannot answer a second call because they have not yet completed the first task. Unless you build your first house well, you will never leave it. *To build your house well is, ironically, to be nudged beyond its doors.*

Remember, Odysseus did a lot of conquering, Abraham a lot of "possessing," Francis a lot of partying, David and Paul a lot of killing, Magdalene a lot of loving, and all of us a lot of ascending and descending, before being ready to go onto the next stage of the journey. Many of us cannot move ahead because we have not done the first task, learned from the last task, or had any of our present accomplishments acknowledged by others. During my fourteen years as chaplain at the Albuquerque jail, I met so many men who remained stymied forever in a teenage psyche, because they had not been able to build their first "house" well, or at all. Nor was there anyone who believed in them. They had usually not been parented well, or had not been given the mirroring that would have secured them within the first half of their own lives.

Yes, we are seduced and fall into the second half of our lives, but a part of that movement is precisely that we have finished the first life tasks, at least in part. We can—and will—move forward as soon as we have completed and lived the previous stage. We almost naturally float forward by the quiet movement of grace when the time is right — and the old agenda shows itself to be insufficient, or even falls apart. All that each of us can do is to live in the now that is given. We cannot rush the process; we can only carry out each stage of our lives to the best of our ability — and then we no longer need to do it anymore! But let's try to describe in greater detail how we build that first house.

CHAPTER 3

THE FIRST HALF OF LIFE

The world is more magical, less predictable, more autonomous, less controllable, more varied, less simple, more infinite, less knowable, more wonderfully troubling than we could have imagined being able to tolerate when we were young.

—JAMES HOLLIS, *FINDING MEANING IN THE SECOND HALF OF LIFE*

I cannot think of a culture in human history, before the present postmodern era, that did not value law, tradition, custom, authority, boundaries, and morality of some clear sort. These containers give us the necessary security, continuity, predictability, impulse control, and ego structure that we need, before the chaos of real life shows up. Healthily conservative people tend to grow up more naturally and more happily than those who receive only free-form, "build it yourself" worldviews, in my studied opinion.

Here is my conviction: *without law in some form, and also without butting up against that law, we cannot move forward easily and naturally.* The rebellions of two-year-olds and teenagers are in our hardwiring, and we have to have something hard and half good to rebel against. We need a worthy opponent against which we test our mettle. As Rilke put it, "When we are only victorious over small things, it leaves us feeling small."

You need a very strong container to hold the contents and contradictions that arrive later in life. You ironically need a very strong ego structure to let go of your ego. You need to struggle with the rules more than a bit before you throw them out. You only internalize values by butting up against external values for a while. All of this builds the strong self that can *positively* obey Jesus—and "die to itself." In fact, far too many (especially women and disadvantaged people) have lived very warped and defeated lives because they tried to give up a self that was not there yet.

This is an important paradox for most of us, and the two sides of this paradox must be made clear for the very health of individuals, families, and cultures. It is crucial for our own civilization right now. We have too many people on the extremes: some make a "sacrificial" and heroic life their whole identity, and end up making everyone else around them sacrifice so that they can be sacrificial and heroic. Others, in selfish rebellion and without any training in letting go, refuse to sacrifice anything. Basically, if you stay in the protected first half of life beyond its natural period, you become a well-disguised narcissist or an adult infant (who is also a narcissist!) — both of whom are often thought to be successful "good old boys" by the mainstream culture. No wonder that Bill Plotkin calls us a "patho-adolescent culture."

The first-half-of-life container, nevertheless, is constructed through impulse controls; traditions; group symbols; family loyalties; basic respect for authority; civil and church laws; and a sense of the goodness, value, and special importance of your country, ethnicity, and religion (as for example, the Jews' sense of their "chosenness"). To quote Archimedes once again, you must have both "a lever and a place to stand" before you can move the world. The educated and sophisticated Western person today has many levers, but almost no solid place on which to stand, with either very weak identities or terribly overstated identities. This tells me we are not doing the first-half-of-life task very well. How can we possibly get to the second?

Most people are trying to build the platform of their lives all by themselves, while working all the new levers at the same time. I think of CEOs, business leaders, soldiers, or parents who have no principled or ethical sense of themselves and end up with some kind of "pick and choose" morality in the pressured moment. This pattern leaves the isolated ego in full control, and surely represents the *hubris* that will precede a lot of impending tragedies. This pattern is all probably predictable when we try to live life backwards and build ourselves a wonderful superstructure before we have laid any real foundations from culture, religion, or tradition. Frankly, it is much easier to begin rather conservative or traditional. I know some of us do not want to hear that.

But I think we all need some help from "the perennial tradition" that has held up over time. We cannot each start at zero, entirely on our own. Life is far too short, and there are plenty of mistakes we do not need to make — and some that we *need* to make. We are parts of social and family ecosystems that are rightly structured to keep us from falling but also, more important, to show us *how* to fall and also *how to learn* from that very falling. Think of the stories of the Brothers Grimm, Hans Christian Anderson, or Laura Ingalls Wilder, most of which circle around a dilemma, a problem, a difficulty, a failure, an evil that begs to be overcome. And always is.

We are not helping our children by always preventing them from what might be necessary falling, because *you learn how to recover from falling by falling!* It is precisely by falling off the bike many times that you eventually learn what the *balance* feels like. The skater pushing both right and left eventually goes where he or she wants to go. People who have never allowed themselves to fall are actually *off balance*, while not realizing it at all. That is why they are so hard to live with. Please think about that for a while.

Law and tradition seem to be necessary in any spiritual system *both to reveal and to limit our basic egocentricity, and to make at least some community, family, and marriage possible.* When you watch ten-year-olds intensely defend the rules of their games, you see what a deep need this is early in life. It structures children's universe and gives them foundational meaning and safety. We cannot flourish early in life inside a totally open field. Children need a good degree of order, predictability, and coherence to grow up well, as Maria Montessori, Rudolf Steiner, and many others have taught. Chaos and chaotic parents will rightly make children cry, withdraw, and rage—both inside and outside.

Cesar Milan, the "dog whisperer," says that dogs cannot be peaceful or teachable if they have no limits set to their freedom and their emotions. They are actually happier and at rest when they live within very clear limits and boundaries, with a "calm and assertive" master. My dog, Venus, is never happier and more teachable than when I am walking her, but on her leash. Could it be the same for humans at certain stages? I suspect so, although it is humiliating to admit it.

Without laws like the Ten Commandments, our existence here on this earth would be pretty pathetic. What if you could not rely on people to tell you the truth? Or not to steal from you? What if we were not expected to respect our parents, and we all started out with cynicism and mistrust of all authority? What if the "I love you" between partners was allowed to mean nothing? What if covetousness, which Rene Girard calls "mimetic rivalry," was encouraged to grow unstopped, as it is in capitalist countries today? Such shapelessness would be the death of any civilization or any kind of trustworthy or happy world. I wonder: Are we there already?

Without laws, human life would be anarchy and chaos, and that chaos would multiply over the generations, like the confused languages of the Tower of Babel (Genesis 11:1–9). We now need basic parenting classes in junior high schools, because so many children have been poorly parented by people who themselves were poorly parented. Far too many people are verbally, physically, sexually, and psychologically abused in our society by people who have no basic relationship skills, and no inner discipline besides.

People who have not been tutored by some "limit situations" in the first half of their life are in no position to parent children; they are usually children themselves. Limit situations, according to the German philosopher Karl Jaspers, are moments, usually accompanied by experiences of dread, responsibility, guilt, or anxiety, in which the human mind confronts its restrictions and boundaries, and allows itself to abandon the false securities of this limitedness, move beyond, one hopes in a positive way, and thus enter new realms of self-consciousness. In other words, we ironically need limit situations and boundaries to grow up. A completely open field does not do the job nearly as well or as quickly. Yahweh was creating a good limit situation for Adam and Eve when he told them *not* to eat the apple, fully knowing that they would.

If you want a job done well, on time, with accountability and no excuses, you had best hire someone who has faced a few limit situations. He or she alone has the discipline, the punctuality, the positive self-image, and the persistence to do a good job. If you want the opposite, hire someone who has been coddled, been given "I Am Special" buttons for doing nothing special, and had all his or her bills paid by others, and whose basic egocentricity has never been challenged or undercut. To be honest, this seems to describe much of the workforce and the student body of America. Many of the papers I receive in summer graduate courses at major universities are embarrassing to read in terms of both style and content, yet these same "adults" are shocked if they do not get an A. This does not bode well for the future of our country.

CONDITIONAL AND UNCONDITIONAL LOVE

In our century we have seen millions give themselves to ideologies of communism, fascism, terrorism, and unfettered capitalism (yes, Wall Street is also an embodiment of our ideology!)—often in angry rebellion either against an oppressive container or because they were given no

soulful container at all. Like never before, we are now seeing the misplaced anger that was at the bottom of many,
if not most, of the social movements of our age. Building on such a negative foundation inevitably produces a
negative building.

None of these "isms" ever create a "civilization of love"
or even positive energy; they are largely theories in the
head and come from the small egoic personality, leaving
the soul bereft, starved, and saddened outside. Without
elders, much of our history has been formed by juniors
reacting, overreacting, and protecting their own temporary
privilege, with no deep-time vision like the Iroquois Nation,
which considered, "What would be good for the next seven
generations?" Compare that to the present "Tea Party"
movement in America.

For any of you who might think this is just old religious
moralizing, I offer the wisdom of Eric Fromm, in his classic
book *The Art of Loving*.[1] He says that the healthiest people
he has known, and those who very often grow up in the
most natural way, are those who, between their two parents
and early authority figures, experienced a combination
of unconditional love along with very conditional and
demanding love! This seems to be true of so many effective
and influential people, like St. Francis, John Muir, Eleanor
Roosevelt, and Mother Teresa, and you can add your own.
I know my siblings and I received conditional love from
our mother and unconditional love from our father. We all

admit now that she served us very well later in life, although we sure fought Mom when we were young. And we were glad Daddy was there to balance her out.

I know this is not the current version of what is psychologically "correct," because we all seem to think we need nothing but unconditional love. Any law, correction, rule, or limitation is another word for conditional love. It is interesting to me that very clear passages describing both God's conditional love and also God's unconditional love are found in the same Scriptures, like Deuteronomy and John's Gospel. The only real biblical promise is that *unconditional love will have the last word!*

The most effective organizations, I am told, have both a "good boss" and a "bad boss," who work closely together. One holds us strongly, while the other speaks hard truth to us and sets clear goals and limits for us. Our naive sense of entitlement and overreaction against all limits to our freedom are not serving us well as parents and marriage partners, not to speak of our needed skills as employees, students, conversationalists, team players, or citizens. It takes the pain of others to produce a humane and just civilization, it seems.

I am convinced that Fromm is wise and correct here, and his wisdom surely matches my own lifetime of observation. It seems we need a foil, a goad, a wall to butt up against to create a proper ego structure and a strong identity. Such a foil is the way we internalize our own deeper

values, educate our feeling function, and dethrone our own
narcissism. Butting up against limits actually teaches us an
awful lot. "I would not have known the meaning of covetousness, if the Law had not said, 'You shall not covet,'"
says St. Paul in his tour de force *against* the law in his letter
to the Romans (7:7)! (For all of his possible neuroses, Paul
was also a spiritual genius; and somehow it is good to know
that neurosis and brilliance can coexist in the same person.)

*Those who whine about parents and authority for too
long invariably remain or become narcissists themselves.* I say
this after working with people on many levels, including
in the jail, as a counselor, and as a confessor. It has been
acceptable for some time in America to remain "wound
identified" (that is, using one's victimhood as one's identity,
one's ticket to sympathy, and one's excuse for not serving),
instead of using the wound to "redeem the world," as we
see in Jesus and many people who turn their wounds into
sacred wounds that liberate both themselves and others.

Oprah would hardly have a TV show if she could not
highlight these many amazing people who have turned their
wounds into gifts for society, and they are often people who
are not overtly religious at all. They often care about others,
and don't want others to be hurt the way they were. It
reminds me of Jesus' story of the two sons, one who said
all the right words, but never acted on these words, and the
other who said the wrong words, but in fact "went to work
in the vineyard." Jesus said that the person who finally acts

and *engages* "does the Father's will," even if he is a tax collector or she a prostitute and does not have the right "belief system" (Matthew 21:28–32). *Jesus seems to often find love in people who might not have received much love themselves. Perhaps their deep longing for it became their capacity to both receive it and give it.* This surely matches my own life experience.

HOLDING A CREATIVE TENSION

Mature people invariably thank their harder parent, law-driven church, kick-ass coach, and most demanding professors—but usually years later. This is a clear sign of having transcended—and included. It is what we should expect fifty- to seventy-year-olds to say, and what you seldom hear from twenty- to forty-year-olds anymore unless they have grown up quite quickly. Some, of course, have also been wounded quite lethally, as in situations of rape or abuse or bullying, and it takes them a longer time to heal and grow.

I am trying to place you and then hold you inside of a very creative tension, if you will allow yourself to be held there. I do promise you it is a *creative* tension, because both law and freedom are necessary for spiritual growth, as Paul says in Romans and Galatians. He learned this from Jesus, who says seven times in a row "The Law says . . . but I say" (Matthew 7:21–48), while also assuring us that he "has not come to throw out the law but to bring it to completion" (7:17). Despite having been directly taught to hold this creative tension, rare is the Christian believer who holds it well. We are usually on bended knee before laws or angrily reacting against them—both immature responses.

Actually, I have seen many Jews, Hindus, and Buddhists do it much better, *but very few Christians have been taught how to live both law and freedom at the same time.* Our Western dualistic minds do not process paradoxes very well. Without a contemplative mind, we do not know how to hold creative tensions. We are better at rushing to judgment and demanding a complete resolution to things before we have learned what they have to teach us. This is not the way of wisdom, and it is the way that people operate in the first half of life.

"Primitive" and native societies might well have held this tension better than we do today.[2] There is much evidence that many traditional societies produced healthy psyches and ego structures by doing the first half of life very well, even if they were not as "developed" or individuated as we are. I have seen this myself among indigenous and "undeveloped" peoples in India, the Philippines, and Latin America. They often seem much less neurotic and anxious than we are, and can deal with failure or loss far, far more easily than we can. Any of you who have been in the barrios, favelas, and townships of the world know how often this is true. Owen Barfield says that they enjoy a kind of simple but transformative "original participation" with reality and with God.

In the Western world, it seems we cannot build prisons fast enough or have enough recovery groups, therapists, or reparenting classes for all of the walking wounded in this very educated, religious, and sophisticated society — which has little respect for limitations and a huge sense of entitlement. How could this happen? How could neuroses and depression be less the exception and more the very norm? Our elderly are seldom elders, it seems to me. When they are true elders, we all fall in love with them.

The presumption has been against law and authority for several centuries now. Tradition or any talk of limits has not been attractive since the protesting Reformation, the unenlightened Enlightenment, or the rise of democracy (all of which were necessary, by the way!). Now we all start our kids in a kind of free fall, and hope that by some good luck or insight they will magically come to wisdom. The ego cannot be allowed to be totally in charge throughout our early years, or it takes over. The entirely open field leaves us the victim of too many options, and the options themselves soon push us around and take control. Law and structure, as fallible as they often are, put up some kind of limits to our infantile grandiosity, and prepare us for helpful relationships with the outer world, which has rights too.

FIRST HALF DONE POORLY

I am also deeply aware of the damage that misuse of law, custom, authority, and tradition has done in human history and to personal development. I know the destructive and immature state that mere reliance on structure and authority has engendered. The anger and blindness it often brings is devastating, because it often takes away both a necessary self-confidence and a necessary self-questioning. We see this in our political debates today, in people's lack of basic self-knowledge (too-quick answers keep you from necessary searching), and in scary fundamentalist thinking in all of the world religions.

Most wars, genocides, and tragedies in history have been waged by unquestioning followers of dominating leaders. Yet there is a strange comfort in staying within the confines of such a leader and his ideologies, even if it leads us to do evil. It frees us from the burden of thinking and from personal responsibility. We are also creatures who love the familiar, the habitual, our own group; and we are all tied deeply to our early conditioning, for good and for ill. Most people will not leave the safety and security of their home base until they have to. Thus the Gospel call, again and again, is to leave home, family, and nets (Mark 1:16–20). Without that necessary separation, order itself, and *my* particular kind of order, will often feel like a kind of "salvation." It has been the most common and bogus substitute for the real liberation offered by mature religion. "Keep the rules, and the rules will keep you!" we were told our first day in the seminary. Franciscans should have known better.

But I am not here to say either-or. I am here to say both-and. It is not just "the exception that proves the rule" but *somehow that the loss or transgression of the rule also proves the importance and purpose of the rule.* You must first eat the fruit of the garden, so you know what it tastes like—and what you are missing if and when you stop eating it. We are perhaps the first generation in history, we postmodern folks, who have the freedom both to know the rules and also to critique the rules at the same time. This is changing everything and evolving consciousness at a rather quick rate.[3]

In the Roman Catholic Church, we are now involved in an enormous example of what some would call "the regressive restoration of persona," a desire to return to the "good old days" when we were supposedly on top, secure, sure of ourselves, and marching together. (I am not persuaded myself, because I lived in those good old days, which were not always so good for a vast majority of people.) We see this especially in young priests, who are seeking the church as their security system and lifelong employer.

Nevertheless, this new tribalism is being found in all of the world religions—a desire for rediscovery of one's roots, one's traditions, one's symbols, one's ethnic identity, and one's own unique identity. Some call it the "identity politics" that rules our country. This is understandable in the midst of massive and scary globalization among six billion people, but it also keeps us trapped at the *bipartisan divide*—and we never achieve the *transpartisan* nature of mature elders. People think that by defeating the other side, they have achieved some high level of truth! Very sad indeed, but that is as far as the angry or fearful dualistic mind can go.

When some have not been able to do the task of the first half of life well, they go back and try to do it again—and then often overdo it! This pattern is usually an inconsistent mix of old-fashioned styles and symbols with very contemporary ideologies of consumerism, technology, militarism, and individualism. This tends to be these individuals' blind spot, which makes them not true conservatives at all. In fact, neoconservatives are usually intense devotees of modern progress and upward mobility in the system, as we see in most Evangelicals, Mormons, and "traditionalist" Catholics. Only groups that have emphasized actual and costly lifestyle changes for themselves, like the Amish, the Shakers, the Mennonites, Catholic Workers, Poor Clares, and the Quakers, can be called true conservatives.

I saw this pattern in my fourteen years as a jail chaplain. The inmates would invariably be overly religious, highly moralistic, and excessively legalistic (believe it or not!), and many overly intellectualized everything. They would do anything to try to compensate for their dashed, maybe never developed, but publicly humiliated criminal self. Here I was the Catholic chaplain, and the last thing I sometimes trusted was a lot of "religious" language and Jesus talk. Again, it was a regressive restoration of a failed first half of life. It seldom works long term.

A recent study pointed out that a strong majority of young men entering seminaries in the last ten to twenty years came from single-parent homes, a high percentage having what we would call "father wounds,"[4] which can take the form of an absent, emotionally unavailable, alcoholic, or even abusive father. This overwhelmingly matches my own experience of working in Catholic seminaries, and of men in jail, the military, or any all-male system. Many of these men were formed in postmodern Europe and America, where almost nothing has been stable or constant or certain since the late 1960s, and even the church was trying to reform itself through the Second Vatican Council.

All has been in flux ever since about 1968. Then add to all of that fifteen years of nonstop public scandal over the issues of pedophilia and cover-up by the hierarchy. Such bishops, priests, and seminarians often had no chance to do the task of the first half of life well. It was a movable famine to grow up in, so they backtracked to do what they should have been able to do first — second! They are out of sequence through no fault of their own. They want a tribe that is both superior and secure — and theirs! Men join a male club, like the church, to get the male energy they never got as sons, or because they accept the male game of "free enterprise" and social advancement. I have often wondered if I did the same. I hope not.

The result is a generation of seminarians and young clergy who are cognitively rigid and "risk adverse"; who want to circle the wagons around their imagined secure and superior group; who seem preoccupied with clothing, titles, perks, and externals of religion; and frankly have little use for the world beyond their own control or explanation. Ecumenism, interfaith dialogue, and social justice are dead issues for them. None of us can dialogue with others until we can calmly and confidently hold our own identity. None of us can know much about second-half-of-life spirituality as long as we are still trying to create the family, the parenting, the security, the order, the pride that we were not given in the first half.

Most of us from my generation cannot go back on this old path, not because it was bad, but *precisely because we already did it, and learned from it*. Unfortunately, we have an entire generation of educators, bishops, and political leaders who are still building their personal towers of success, and therefore have little ability to elder the young or challenge the beginners. In some ways, they are still beginners themselves. Self-knowledge is dismissed as psychology, love as "feminine softness," critical thinking as disloyalty, while law, ritual, and priestcraft have become a compulsive substitute for actual divine encounter or honest relationship. This does not bode well for the future of any church or society.

So let's look at a way through all of this, because *spiritually speaking, there are no dead ends.* God will use this too — somehow — and draw all of us toward the Great Life. But there is a way to move ahead more naturally, if we can recognize a common disguise and dead end.

DISCHARGING YOUR LOYAL SOLDIER

In his work at his Animas Institute in Durango, Colorado, Bill Plotkin takes people on long fasts and vision quests in nature. His work offers a very specific and truth-filled plan for moving from what he calls an "ego centric" worldview to a "soul centric" worldview.[5] Like me, Plotkin is saddened by how much of our world stays at the egocentric first stage of life. His work reveals a historical situation in post–World War II Japan that demonstrates how people could be helped to move from the identity of the first half of life to the growth of the second half. In this situation, some Japanese communities had the savvy to understand that many of their returning soldiers were not fit or prepared to reenter civil or humane society. Their only identity for their formative years had been to be a "loyal soldier" to their country; they needed a broader identity to once again rejoin their communities as useful citizens.[6]

So these Japanese communities created a communal ritual whereby a soldier was publicly thanked and praised effusively for his service to the people. After this was done at great length, an elder would stand and announce with authority something to this effect: "The war is now over! The community needs you to let go of what has served you and served us well up to now. The community needs you to return as a man, a citizen, and something beyond a soldier." In our men's work, we call this process "discharging your loyal soldier."

This kind of closure is much needed for most of us at the end of all major transitions in life. Because we have lost any sense of the need for such rites of passage, most of our people have no clear crossover to the second half of their own lives. No one shows us the stunted and limited character of the worldview of the first half of life, so we just continue with more of the same. The Japanese were wise enough to create clear closure, transition, and possible direction. Western people are a *ritually starved* people, and in this are different than most of human history. Even the church's sacraments are overwhelmingly dedicated to keeping us loyally inside the flock and tied to the clergy, loyal soldiers of the church. There is little talk of journeys outward or onward, the kind of journeys Jesus called people to go on.

The state also wants loyal patriots and citizens, not thinkers, critics, or citizens of a larger world. No wonder we have so much depression and addiction, especially among the elderly, and also among the churched. Their full life has been truncated with the full cooperation of both church and state.

The loyal soldier is similar to the "elder son" in Jesus' parable of the prodigal son. His very loyalty to strict meritocracy, to his own entitlement, to obedience and loyalty to his father, keeps him from the very "celebration" that same father has prepared, even though he begs the son to come to the feast (Luke 15:25–32). We have no indication he ever came! What a judgment this is on first-stage religion, and it comes straight from the boss. He makes the same point in his story of the Pharisee and the tax collector (Luke 18:9–14), in which one is loyal and observant and deemed wrong by Jesus, and the other has not obeyed the law—yet is deemed "at rights with God." This is classic "reverse theology" meant to subvert our usual merit-badge thinking. Both the elder son and the Pharisee are good loyal religious soldiers, exactly what most of us in the church were told to be, yet Jesus says that both of them missed the major point.

The voice of our loyal soldier gets us through the first half of life safely, teaching us to look both ways before we cross the street, to have enough impulse control to avoid addictions and compulsive emotions, to learn the sacred "no" to ourselves that gives us dignity, identity, direction, significance, and boundaries. We *must* learn these lessons to get off to a good start! It is far easier to begin life with a conservative worldview and respect for traditions. It gives you an initial sense of "place" and is much more effective in the long run, even if it just gives you "a goad to kick against" (Acts 26:14). Many just fall in love with their first place and position, as an extension of themselves, and spend their whole life building a white picket fence around it.

Without a loyal soldier protecting us up to age thirty, the world's prisons and psych wards would be even more overcrowded than they are. Testosterone, addiction, ego, promiscuity, and vanity would win out in most of our lives. Without our loyal soldier, we would all be aimless and shapeless, with no home base and no sustained relationships, because there would be no "me" at home to have a relationship with. Lots of levers, but no place to stand.

Paradoxically, your loyal soldier gives you so much security and validation that you may confuse his voice with the very voice of God. *If this inner and critical voice has kept you safe for many years as your inner voice of authority, you may end up not being able to hear the real voice of God.* (Please read that sentence again for maximum effect!) The loyal soldier is the voice of all your early authority figures. His or her ability to offer shame, guilt, warnings, boundaries, and self-doubt is the gift that never stops giving. Remember, it can be a feminine voice too; but it is not the "still, small voice" of God (1 Kings 19:13) that *gives us our power instead of always taking our power*.

The loyal soldier cannot get you to the second half of life. He does not even understand it. He has not been there. He can help you "get through hell," with the early decisions that demand black-and-white thinking; but then you have to say good-bye when you move into the subtlety of midlife and later life. The Japanese were correct, as were the Greeks. Odysseus is a loyal soldier for the entire Odyssey, rowing his boat as only a hero can—until the blind prophet tells him there is more, and to put down his oar. If you ever read the *Divine Comedy,* note that Dante lets go of Virgil, who had accompanied him through Hades and Purgatory, knowing now that only Beatrice can lead him into Paradise.

Virgil is the first-half-of-life man; Beatrice is the second-half-of-life woman. In the first half of life, we fight the devil and have the illusion and inflation of "winning" now and then; in the second half of life, we always lose because we are invariably fighting God. *The first battles solidify the ego and create a stalwart loyal soldier; the second battles defeat the ego because God always wins*. No wonder so few want to let go of their loyal soldier; no wonder so few have the faith to grow up. The ego hates losing, even to God.

The loyal soldier is largely the same thing that Freud was describing with his concept of the superego, which he said usually substitutes for any real adult formation of conscience. The superego feels like God, because people have had nothing else to guide them. Such a bogus conscience is a terrible substitute for authentic morality. What reveals its bogus character is its major resistance to change and growth, and its substituting of small, low-cost moral issues for the real ones that ask *us* to change, instead of always trying to change other people. Jesus called it "straining out gnats while swallowing camels" (Matthew 23:24). It is much more common than I ever imagined, until I myself began to serve as a confessor and spiritual director.

There is a deeper voice of God, which you must learn to *hear and obey* in the second half of life. It will sound an awful lot like the voices of risk, of trust, of surrender, of soul, of "common sense," of destiny, of love, of an intimate stranger, of your deepest self, of soulful "Beatrice." The true faith journey only begins at this point. Up to now everything is mere preparation. Finally, we have a container strong enough to hold the contents of our real life, which is always filled with contradictions and adventures and immense challenges. *Psychological wholeness and spiritual holiness never exclude the problem from the solution. If it is wholeness, then it is always paradoxical, and holds both the dark and light sides of things.* Wholeness and holiness will always stretch us beyond our small comfort zone. How could they not?

So God, life, and destiny have to loosen the loyal soldier's grasp on your soul, which up to now has felt like the only "you" that you know and the only authority that there is. Our loyal soldier normally begins to be discharged somewhere between the ages of thirty-five and fifty-five, if it happens at all; before that it is usually mere rebellion or iconoclasm.

To let go of the loyal soldier will be a severe death, and an exile from your first base. You will feel similar to Isaiah before he was sent into exile in Babylon, "In the noontime of my life, I was told to depart for the gates of Hades. Surely I am deprived of the rest of my years" (38:10). Discharging your loyal soldier will be necessary to finding authentic inner authority, or what Jeremiah promised as "the law written in your heart" (31:33). First-half-of-life folks will seldom have the courage to go forward at this point unless they have a guide, a friend, a Virgil, a Teiresias, a Beatrice, a soul friend, or a stumbling block to guide them toward the goal. There are few in our religious culture who understand the necessity of mature internalized conscience, so wise guides are hard to find. You will have many more Aarons building you golden calves than Moseses leading you on any exodus.

Normally we will not discharge our loyal soldier until he shows himself to be wanting, incapable, inadequate for the real issues of life—as when we confront love, death, suffering, subtlety, sin, mystery, and so on. It is another form of the falling and dying that we keep talking about. The world mythologies all point to places like Hades, Sheol, hell, purgatory, the realm of the dead. *Maybe these are not so much the alternative to heaven as the necessary path to heaven.*

Even Jesus, if we are to believe the "Apostle's Creed" of the church, "descended into hell" before he ascended into heaven. Isn't it strange how we missed that? Every initiation rite I studied worldwide was always about "dying before you die." When you first discharge your loyal soldier, it will feel like a loss of faith or loss of self. *But it is only the death of the false self, and is often the very birth of the soul.* Instead of being ego driven, you will begin to be soul drawn. The wisdom and guidance you will need to get you across this chasm will be like Charon ferrying you across the river Styx, or Hermes guiding the soul across all scary boundaries. These are your authentic soul friends, and we now sometimes call them spiritual directors or elders. Celtic Christianity called them *anam chara.*

Remember that Hercules, Orpheus, Aeneas, Psyche, and our Odysseus all traveled into realms of the dead — and returned! Most mythologies include a descent into the underworld at some point. Jesus, as we said, also "descended into hell," and only on the third day did he "ascend into heaven." Most of life is lived, as it were, on the "first and second days," the threshold days when transformation is happening but we do not know it yet. In men's work we call this *liminal space.*[7]

St. John of the Cross taught that God has to work in the soul *in secret* and *in darkness,* because *if we fully knew what was happening, and what Mystery/transformation/ God/grace will eventually ask of us, we would either try to take charge or stop the whole process.*[8] No one oversees his or her own demise willingly, even when it is the false self that is dying.

God has to undo our illusions secretly, as it were, when we are not watching and not in perfect control, say the mystics. That is perhaps why the best word for God is actually *Mystery*. We move forward in ways that we do not even understand and through the quiet workings of time and grace. When we get there, we are never sure just how it happened, and God does not seem to care who gets the credit, as long as our growth continues. As St. Gregory of Nyssa already said in the fourth century, "Sin happens whenever we refuse to keep growing."

CHAPTER 4

THE TRAGIC SENSE OF LIFE

In the deeps are the violence and terror of which psychology has warned us. But if you ride these monsters down, if you drop with them farther over the world's rim, you find what our sciences cannot locate or name, the substrate, the ocean or matrix or ether which buoys the rest, which gives goodness its power for good, and evil its power of evil, the unified field: our complex and inexplicable caring for each other, and for our life together here. This is given. It is not learned.

—ANNIE DILLARD, *TEACHING A STONE TO TALK*

The exact phrase, "the tragic sense of life," was first popularized in the early twentieth century by the Spanish philosopher Miguel de Unamuno, who courageously told his European world that they had distorted the meaning of faith by aligning it with the Western philosophy of "progress" rather than with what he saw as rather evident in the Judeo-Christian Scriptures.[1] Jesus and the Jewish prophets were fully at home with the tragic sense of life, and it made the shape and nature of reality very different for them, for Unamuno, and maybe still for us.

By this clear and honest phrase, I understand Unamuno to mean that life is not, nor ever has been, a straight line forward. According to him, life is characterized much more by exception and disorder than by total or perfect order. Life, as the biblical tradition makes clear, is both loss and renewal, death and resurrection, chaos and healing at the same time; life seems to be a collision of opposites. Unamuno equates the notion of faith with trust in an underlying life force so strong that it even includes death. Faith also includes reason, but is a larger category than reason for Unamuno. Truth is not always about pragmatic problem solving and making things "work," but about reconciling contradictions. Just because something might have some dire effects does not mean it is not true or even good. Just because something pleases people does not make it true either. Life is inherently tragic, and that is the truth that only faith, but not our seeming logic, can accept. This is my amateur and very partial summary of the thought of this great Spanish philosopher.

THE "TRAGIC" NATURAL WORLD

In our time, it is quantum physics that shows how true Unamuno's explanation might really be. Most of us were formed by Newtonian worldviews in which everything had a clear cause and equal effect, what might be called an "if-then" worldview. All causality was clear and defined. The truth we are now beginning to respect is that the universe seems to proceed through a web of causes, just as human motivation does, producing ever-increasing diversity, multiplicity, dark holes, dark matter, death and rebirth, loss and renewal in different forms, and yes even violence, the continual breaking of the rules of "reason" that make wise people look for more all-embracing rules and a larger "logic."

Nature is much more disorder than order, more multiplicity than uniformity, with the greatest disorder being death itself! In the spiritual life, and now in science, we learn much more by honoring and learning from the exceptions than by just imposing our previous certain rules to make everything fit. You can see perhaps what Jesus and Paul both meant by telling us to honor "the least of the brothers and sisters" (Matthew 25:40; 1 Corinthians 12:22–25) and to "clothe them with the greatest care." It is those creatures and those humans who are on the edge of what we have defined as normal, proper, or good who often have the most to teach us. They tend to reveal the shadow and mysterious side of things. Such constant exceptions make us revisit the so-called rule and what we call normal—and recalibrate! The exceptions keep us humble and searching, and not rushing toward resolution to allay our anxiety.

Our daily experience of this world is almost nothing like Plato's world of universal and perfect forms and ideas; it is always filled with huge diversity, and variations on every theme from neutrino light inside of darkness, to male

seahorses that bear their young, to the most extraordinary
flowers that only open at night for no one to see. Jesus had no
trouble with the exceptions, whether they were prostitutes,
drunkards, Samaritans, lepers, Gentiles, tax collectors, or
wayward sheep. He ate with outsiders regularly, to the cha-
grin of the church stalwarts, who always love their version
of order over any compassion toward the exceptions. Just
the existence of a single mentally challenged or mentally ill
person should make us change any of our theories about
the necessity of some kind of correct thinking as the definition of "salvation." Yet we have a history of excluding and
torturing people who do not "think" right.

I remember the final words of my professor of church
history, a very orthodox priest theologian, who said as he
walked out of the classroom after our four years of study
with him, "Well, after all is said and done, remember that
church practice has been more influenced by Plato than
by Jesus." We reeled in astonishment, but the four years
of history had spoken for themselves. What he meant, of
course, was that we invariably prefer the universal synthesis,
the answer that settles all the dust and resolves every
question—even when it is not entirely true—over the
mercy and grace of God. Jesus did not seem to teach that
one size fits all, but instead that his God adjusts to the
vagaries and failures of the moment. This ability to adjust
to human disorder and failure is named God's providence
or compassion. *Every time God forgives us, God is saying that*

God's own rules do not matter as much as the relationship that God wants to create with us. Just the Biblical notion of absolute forgiveness, once experienced, should be enough to make us trust and seek and love God.

But we humans have a hard time with the specific, the concrete, the individual, the anecdotal story, which hardly ever fits the universal mold. So we pretend. Maybe that is why we like and need humor, which invariably reveals these inconsistencies. In Franciscan thinking, this specific, individual, concrete thing is always God's work and God's continuing choice, precisely in its uniqueness, not in its uniformity. Duns Scotus called it "thisness." Christians believe that "incarnation" showed itself in one unique specific person, Jesus. It becomes his pattern too, as he leaves the ninety-nine for the one lost sheep (Matthew 18:12–14). Some theologians have called this divine pattern of incarnation "the scandal of the particular." Our mind, it seems, is more pleased with universals: never-broken, always-applicable rules and patterns that allow us to predict and control things. This is good for science, but lousy for religion.

The universe story and the human story are a play of forces rational and nonrational, conscious and unconscious; of fate and fortune, nature and nurture. Forces of good and evil play out their tragedies and their graces—leading us to catastrophes, backtracking, mutations, transgressions, regroupings, enmities, failures, mistakes, and impossible dilemmas. (We will get to the good part later!) Did you know that the Greek word for *tragedy* means "goat story"? The Odyssey is a primal goat story, where poor Odysseus keeps going forward and backward, up and down — but mostly down — all the way home to Ithaca.

Each of these experiences is meant to lead us to a new knowledge and a movement "forward" in some sense, yet it is always a humbled knowledge. *Greek hubris was precisely the refusal to be humbled by what should have been humbling.* Notice how no American president can fully admit that his war or his policies were wrong — ever. Popes and clergy have not been known for apologizing. Such pride and delusion was the core of every Greek tragedy — and became the precise staging for the transformation of Jesus himself into a new kind of life that we called the Risen Christ.

The Gospel was able to accept that life is tragic, but then graciously added that we can survive and will even grow from this tragedy. This is the great turnaround! It all depends on whether we are willing to see down as up; or as Jung put it, that "where you stumble and fall, there you find pure gold." Lady Julian put it even more poetically: "First there is the fall, and then we recover from the fall. Both are the mercy of God!"

We should have been prepared for this pattern, given that the whole drama was set in motion by the "transgression" of Adam and Eve, and then the whole world was redeemed, say many Christians, by an act of violent murder! If God has not learned to draw straight with crooked lines, God is not going to be drawing very many lines at all. *Judeo-Christian salvation history is an integrating, using, and forgiving of this tragic sense of life.* Judeo-Christianity includes the problem inside the solution and as part of the solution. The genius of the biblical revelation is that it refuses to deny the dark side of things, but forgives failure and integrates falling to achieve its only promised wholeness, which is much of the point of this whole book.

Jesus is never upset at sinners (check it out!); he is only upset with people who do not think they are sinners! Jesus was fully at home with this tragic sense of life. He lived and rose inside it. I am now personally convinced that Jesus' ability to find a higher order inside constant disorder is the very heart of his message — and why true Gospel, as rare as it might be, still heals and renews all that it touches.

Jesus found and named the unified field beneath all the contradictions, which Annie Dillard spoke of in the epigraph above. If we do not find that unified field, "our complex and inexplicable caring for each other," or what Buddhists call the Great Compassion, there is no healing to life's inconsistencies and contradictions. *Religion is always about getting you back and down into the unified field, where you started anyway.*

THE GREAT TURNAROUND

In the divine economy of grace, sin and failure become the base metal and raw material for the redemption experience itself. Much of organized religion, however, tends to be peopled by folks who have a mania for some ideal order, which is never true, so they are seldom happy or content. It makes you anal retentive after a while, to use Freud's rude phrase, because you can never be happy with life as it is, which is always filled with handicapped people, mentally unstable people, people of "other" and "false" religions, irritable people, gay people, and people of totally different customs and traditions. Not to speak of *wild* nature, which we have not loved very well up to now. Organized religion has not been known for its inclusiveness or for being very comfortable with diversity. Yet pluriformity, multiplicity, and diversity is the only world there is! It is rather amazing that we can miss, deny, or ignore what is in plain sight everywhere.

Sin and salvation are correlative terms. Salvation is not sin perfectly avoided, as the ego would prefer; but in fact, *salvation is sin turned on its head and used in our favor*. That is how transformative divine love is. If this is not the pattern, what hope is there for 99.9 percent of the world? We eventually discover that the same passion which leads us away from God can also lead us back to God and to our true selves. That is one reason I have valued and taught the Enneagram for almost forty years now.[2] Like few other spiritual tools, it illustrates this transformative truth. Once you see that your "sin" and your gift are two sides of the same coin, you can never forget it. It preserves religion from any arrogance and denial. The only people who do not believe that the Enneagram is true are those who do not understand it or have never used it well.

God seems to be about "turning" our loves around (in Greek, *meta-noia*), and using them toward the Great Love that is their true object. All lesser loves are training wheels, which are good in themselves, but still training wheels. Many of the healing stories in the New Testament are rather clear illustrations of this message and pattern. Jesus says this specifically of "the woman who was a sinner": "Her sins, her many sins, must have been forgiven her, or she could not have shown such great love" (Luke 7:47). It seems that her false attempts at love became the school and stepping-stones to "such great love."

We clergy have gotten ourselves into the job of "sin management" instead of sin transformation. "If you are not perfect, then *you* are doing something wrong," we have taught people. We have blamed the victim, or have had little pity for victims, while daring to worship a victim image of God. Our mistakes are something to be pitied and healed much more than hated, denied, or perfectly avoided. I do not think you should get rid of your sin until you have learned what it has to teach you. Otherwise, it will only return in new forms, as Jesus says of the "unclean spirit" that returns to the house all "swept and tidied" (Luke 11:24–26); then he rightly and courageously says that "the last state of the house will be worse than the first."

One could say that the tragedy, the "goat stories" of racism, slavery, sexism, the Crusades, the Inquisition, and the two World Wars, all of which emerged in and were tolerated by Christian Europe, are a stunning manifestation of our disillusionment and disgust with ourselves and one another, when we could not make the world right and perfectly ordered, as we were told it should be. We could not love the imperfection within ourselves or the natural world, so how could we possibly build any bridges toward Jews, Muslims, people of color, women, sinners, or even other Christians? None of them fit into the "order" we had predecided on. We had to kill, force, imprison, torture, and enslave as we pursued our colonization of the rest of the world, along with the planet itself. We did not carry the cross, the tragic sense of life, but we became expert instead at imposing tragedies on others. Forgive my anger, but we must say it.

Philosophers and social engineers have promised us various utopias, with no room for error, but the Jewish Scriptures, which are full of anecdotes of destiny, failure, sin, and grace, *offer almost no self-evident philosophical or theological conclusions that are always true.*[3] The Pentateuch, the first five books of the Bible, are an amalgam of at least four different sources and theologies (Yahwistic, Eloistic, Deuteronomic, and Priestly). We even have four, often conflicting versions of the life of Jesus in Matthew, Mark, Luke, and John. There is not one clear theology of God, Jesus, or history presented, despite our attempt to pretend there is. The only consistent pattern I can find is that all the books of the Bible seem to agree that *somehow God is with us and we are not alone*. God and Jesus' only job description is one of constant renewal of bad deals.

The tragic sense of life is ironically not tragic at all, at least in the Big Picture. Living in such deep time, connected to past and future, prepares us for necessary suffering, keeps us from despair about our own failure and loss, and ironically offers us a way through it all. We are merely joining the great parade of humanity that has walked ahead of us and will follow after us. The tragic sense of life is not unbelief, pessimism, fatalism, or cynicism. It is just *ultimate and humiliating realism,* which for some reason demands a lot of forgiveness of almost everything. Faith is simply to trust the real, and to trust that God is found within it—even before we change it. This is perhaps our major stumbling stone, the price we must pay to keep the human heart from closing down and to keep the soul open for something more.

CHAPTER 5

STUMBLING OVER THE STUMBLING STONE

*God is both sanctuary and stumbling stone,
Yahweh is a rock that brings Israel down, the
Lord is a trap and snare for the people.*
—ISAIAH 8:14

*We would rather be ruined than changed. We
would rather die in our dread than climb the
cross of the present and let our illusions die.*
—W. H. AUDEN

Sooner or later, if you are on any classic "spiritual schedule," some event, person, death, idea, or relationship will enter your life that you simply cannot deal with, using your present skill set, your acquired knowledge, or your strong willpower. Spiritually speaking, you will be, you must be, led to the edge of your own private resources. At that point you will stumble over a necessary stumbling stone, as Isaiah calls it; or to state it in our language here, you will and you must "lose" at something. This is the only way that Life-Fate-God-Grace-Mystery can get you to change, let go of your egocentric preoccupations, and go

on the further and larger journey. I wish I could say this
was not true, but it is darn near absolute in the spiritual
literature of the world.

There is no practical or compelling reason to leave
one's present comfort zone in life. Why should you or
would you? Frankly, none of us do unless and until we
have to. The invitation probably has to be unexpected and
unsought. If we seek spiritual heroism ourselves, the old
ego is just back in control under a new name. There would
not really be any change at all, but only disguise. Just bogus
"self-improvement" on our own terms.

Any attempt to engineer or plan your own enlightenment is doomed to failure because it will be ego driven. You
will see only what you have already decided to look for,
and you cannot see what you are not ready or told to look
for. So failure and humiliation force you to look where you
never would otherwise. What an enigma! Self-help courses
of any type, including this one if it is one, will help you only
if they teach you to pay attention to life itself. "God comes
to you disguised as your life," as my friend Paula D'Arcy so
wisely says.

So we *must* stumble and fall, I am sorry to say. And
that does not mean reading about falling, as you are doing
here. We must actually be out of the driver's seat for a
while, or we will never learn how to *give up* control to the
Real Guide. It is the necessary pattern. This kind of falling
is what I mean by necessary suffering, which I will try to

describe in the next chapter. It is well dramatized by Paul's fall on the Damascus Road, where he hears the voice "Why are you hurting yourself by kicking against the goad?" (Acts 26:14). The goad or cattle prod is the symbol of both the encouragement forward and our needless resistance to it, which only wounds us further.

It seems that in the spiritual world, we do not really find something until we first lose it, ignore it, miss it, long for it, choose it, and personally find it again—but now on a new level. Three of the parables of Jesus are about losing something, searching for it anew with some effort, finding it, and in each case throwing a big party afterwards. A sheep, a coin, a son are all lost and found in Luke 15, followed by the kind of inner celebration that comes with any new "realization" (when something has become *real* for you). Almost every one of Odysseus's encounters coming home from Troy are losses of some type—his men, his control, his power, his time, his memory, his fame, the boat itself. Falling, losing, failing, transgression, and sin are the pattern, I am sorry to report. Yet they all lead toward home.

In the end, we do not so much reclaim what we have lost as discover a significantly new self in and through the process. Until we are led to the limits of our present game plan, and find it to be insufficient, we will not search out or find the real source, the deep well, or the constantly flowing stream. Alcoholics Anonymous calls it the Higher Power.

Jesus calls this Ultimate Source the "living water" at the bottom of the well, to the woman who keeps filling and refilling her own little bucket (John 4:10–14).

There must be, and, if we are honest, there always will be at least *one situation in our lives that we cannot fix, control, explain, change, or even understand*. For Jesus and for his followers, the crucifixion became the dramatic symbol of that necessary and absurd stumbling stone. Yet we have no positive theology of such necessary suffering, for the most part. Many Christians even made the cross into a mechanical "substitutionary atonement theory" to fit into their quid pro quo worldview, instead of suffering its inherent tragedy, as Jesus did himself. They still want some kind of order and reason, instead of cosmic significance and soulful seeing.[1]

We, like the ox and St. Paul, largely still "kick against the goad," instead of listening to and learning from the goads of everyday life. Christians who read such passages were still not able to see that the goads were somehow necessary or even good. Suffering does not solve any problem mechanically as much as it reveals the constant problem that we are to ourselves, and opens up new spaces within us for learning and loving. Here Buddhism was much more observant than Christianity, which made even the suffering of Jesus into God's attempt to solve some cosmic problem — which God had largely created to begin with! The cross solved our problem by first revealing our real problem — our universal pattern of scapegoating and sacrificing others. The cross exposes forever the "scene of our crime."

In the tale of Odysseus and in other stories from world mythology, the theme of loss and humiliation was constant and unrelenting, variously presented as the dragon, the sea monster, Scylla and Charybdis, an imprisonment, plague or illness, a falling into hell, the sirens, a storm, darkness, a shipwreck, the lotus eaters, the state of fatherlessness or orphanhood, homelessness, being stranded on an island, blindness, and often the powerless state of poverty and penury.

Sometimes it seems that half of the fairy tales of the world are some form of Cinderella, ugly duckling, or poor boy story, telling of the little person who has no power or possessions who ends up being king or queen, prince or princess. We write it off as wishful dreaming, when it is actually the foundational pattern of disguise or amnesia, loss, and recovery. Every Beauty is sleeping, it seems, before it can meet its Prince. The duckling must be "ugly," or there will be no story. The knight errant must be wounded, or he will never even know what the Holy Grail is, much less find it. Jesus must be crucified, or there can be no resurrection. It is written in our hardwiring, but can only be heard at the soul level. It will usually be resisted and opposed at the ego level.

My own spiritual father, Francis of Assisi, says in his *Testament* that when he kissed the leper, "What before

had been nauseating to me became sweetness and life."
He marks that moment as the moment of his conversion
and the moment when he "left the world." The old game
could not, would not work anymore. That seems to have
been the defining moment when he tasted his own insuf-
ficiency, and started drawing from a different and larger
source—and found it sufficient—apparently even more
than sufficient. It made him into the classic Christian saint.
The leper was his goad, and he learned not to kick against
it, but actually to kiss it. That is the pattern, just as you
will sometimes hear from recovering addicts who end up
thanking God for their former drinking, gambling, or violence. They invariably say that it was a huge price to pay,
but nothing less would have broken down their false self
and opened them to love.

   I can only think of the many men and women I met
during my fourteen years as a jail chaplain here in New
Mexico. No one taught them the necessary impulse control and delay of gratification, which is the job of a good
parent. With poor identity, weak boundaries, or little inherent sense of their dignity, they allowed themselves to be
destroyed—and to destroy others—by drugs, promiscuity,
addictive relationships, alcohol, violence, or abuse. Then
the enforced and cruel order of the jail was supposed to
serve as their reparenting course, but now the lesson was so
much harder to learn because of all the inner scarring and
resentments toward all authority and toward themselves.

If you do not do the task of the first half of life well, you have almost no ability to rise up from the stumbling stone. You just stay down and defeated, or you waste your time kicking against the goad. There has been nothing to defeat your "infantile grandiosity," as Dr. Robert Moore wisely calls it.[2] In much of urban and Western civilization today, with no proper tragic sense of life, we try to believe that it is all upward and onward—and by ourselves. It works for so few, and it cannot serve us well in the long run—because it is not true. It is an inherently win-lose game, and more and more people find themselves on the losing side. If the Gospel is indeed gospel ("good news"), then it has to be win-win, and a giant victory for both God and us.

Almost all of us end up being casualties of this constantly recurring Greek *hubris*. Some even appear to make it to the "top," but there is usually little recognition of the many shoulders they stood on to move there, the many gratuitous circumstances that made it possible for them to arrive there, and sometimes the necks they have stood on to stay there. Some who get to the top have the savvy to recognize that there is nothing up there that lasts or satisfies. Far too many just stay at the bottom of their own lives and try to overcompensate in all kinds of futile and self-defeating ways.

I am sure many slaveholders in the South were "self-made men" and perhaps never in their entire lives had to face a situation where they did not "succeed." Such a refusal to fall kept them from awareness, empathy, and even basic human compassion. The price they paid for such succeeding was an inability to allow, join, or enjoy "the general dance." They "gained the whole world, but lost their soul," as Jesus put it. They did their survival dance, but never got to the sacred dance, which by necessity includes everybody else. If it is a sacred dance, it is always the general dance too.

CHAPTER 6

NECESSARY SUFFERING

*Anyone who wants to save his life, must lose
it. Anyone who loses her life will find it. What
gain is there if you win the whole world and
lose your very self? What can you offer in
exchange for your one life?*
—MATTHEW 16:25–26

*If anyone comes to me and does not hate his
father and mother, his wife and children,
his brothers and sisters—yes, even his own
life—he cannot be my disciple.*
—LUKE 14:26

Carl Jung said that so much unnecessary suffering comes into the world because people will not accept the "legitimate suffering" that comes from being human. In fact, he said neurotic behavior is usually the result of refusing that legitimate suffering! Ironically, this refusal of the necessary pain of being human brings to the person ten times more suffering in the long run. It is no surprise that the first and always unwelcome message in male initiation rites is "life is hard." We really are our own worst enemy when we deny this.

To explain why I begin this chapter on necessary suffering with two hard-hitting quotes from Jesus of Nazareth, let me explain a bit about myself. I must start with my birth relationship with Catholic Christianity (I presume you know that I have been a priest for forty years, and a Franciscan for almost fifty), because in many ways it has been the church that has taught me—in ways that it did not plan—the message of necessary suffering. It taught me by itself being a bearer of the verbal message, then a holding tank, and finally a living crucible of necessary (and sometimes unnecessary!) suffering.

A crucible, as you know, is a vessel that holds molten metal in one place long enough to be purified and clarified. Church membership requirements, church doctrine, and church morality force almost all issues to an inner boiling point, where you are forced to face important issues at a much deeper level to survive as a Catholic or a Christian, or even as a human. I think this is probably true of any religious community, if it is doing its job. *Before the truth "sets you free," it tends to make you miserable.*

The Christian truth, and Jesus as its spokesman, is the worldview that got me started, that formed me and thrilled me, even though the very tangent that it sent me on made me often critical of much of organized Christianity.

In some ways, that is totally as it should be, because I was able to criticize organized religion from within, by its own Scriptures, saints, and sources, and not by merely cultural, unbelieving, or rational criteria. That is probably the only way you can fruitfully criticize anything, it seems to me. You must unlock spiritual things from the inside, and not by throwing rocks from outside, which is always too easy and too self-aggrandizing.

Eventually I found myself held inside Christianity's inherent tensions. Catholicism became for me, and I think as it has for many, *a crucible and thus a unified field*. Which is why it is very hard to be a "former" Catholic, once you really get its incarnational and inherently mystical worldview. I here use Einstein's term "unified field" to describe *that single world of elementary forces, principles, and particles that he assumed held together the entire universe of space-time*. Einstein said that he spent his life looking for this unified field.

Although its vision is often time bound and its vocabulary very "in house" (if you don't use our words, and our definitions of those words, many Catholics hardly know how to talk to you), I still find that Big Picture Catholicism is often precisely that — very "catholic" and all embracing — with room for head, heart, body, soul, and history. For all its failures, it is no surprise that the Catholic worldview (note that I am not saying the "Roman" worldview) continues to produce Teilhard de Chardins, Mother Teresas, Thomas Mertons, Edith Steins, Cesar Chavezes, Cory Aquinos, Mary Robinsons, Rowan Williamses, Desmond Tutus, and Dorothy Days. I like to call it "incarnational mysticism." Once you get it, there is no going backward, because nothing is any better.

The pedestrian and everyday church has remained a cauldron of transformation for me by holding me inside both the dark and the light side of almost everything, and by teaching me nondualistic thinking to survive. It has also shown me that neither I nor the churches themselves really live much of the real Gospel—at least enough to actually change our present lifestyles! It is just too big a message. Refusing to split and deny reality keeps me in regular touch with my own shadow self, and much more patient with the rather evident shadow of the church. I see the exact same patterns in every other group, so my home base is as good a place to learn shadowboxing as anywhere else, and often better than most. Intellectual rigor, a social conscience (at least on paper), and a mystical vision are there for the taking. Catholicism is the "one true church" only when it points beyond itself to the "one true Mystery," and offers itself as the training ground for both human liberation and divine union. Many other religious groups do the same, however, and sometimes much better.

ALL CREATION "GROANS" (ROMANS 8:22)

Creation itself, the natural world, already "believes" the Gospel, and lives the pattern of death and resurrection, even if unknowingly. The natural world "believes" in necessary suffering as the very cycle of life: just observe the daily dying of the sun so all things on this planet can live, the total change of the seasons, the plants and trees along with it, the violent world of animal predators and prey. My own sweet black Lab, Venus, today killed a little groundhog, and brought it to me expecting approval. How could she think this was wonderful when I thought it was terrible? She dropped it with disappointment when she saw my eyes. Only the human species absents itself from the agreed-on pattern and the general dance of life and death. What Venus had done would be disastrous only if I want to be perfectly rational and "progressive."

Necessary suffering goes on every day, seemingly without question. As I write this in the deserts of Arizona, I just read that only one saguaro cactus seed out of a quarter of a million seeds ever makes it even to early maturity, and even fewer after that. Most of nature seems to totally accept major loss, gross inefficiency, mass extinctions, and short life spans as the price of life at all. Feeling that sadness, and even its full absurdity, ironically pulls us into the general dance, the unified field, an ironic and deep gratitude for what *is* given—with no necessity and so gratuitously. All beauty is gratuitous. So whom can we blame when it seems to be taken away? Grace seems to be at the foundation of everything.

This creative tension between wonderful and terrible is named so well by Gerard Manley Hopkins, as only poets can. Even the long title of his poem reveals his acceptance of the ever-changing flow of Heraclites and also his trust in the final outcome: "That Nature Is a Heraclitean Fire and of the Comfort of the Resurrection."

> Flesh fade, and mortal trash
> fall to the residuary worm; world's wildfire, leave but ash:
> In a flash, at a trumpet crash,
> I am all at once what Christ is, since he was what I
>   am, and
> This Jack, joke, poor potsherd, patch, matchwood,
>   immortal diamond,
> Is immortal diamond.[1]

The resolution of earthly embodiment and divinization is what I call *incarnational mysticism*. As has been said many times, there are finally only two subjects in all of literature and poetry: love and death. Only that which is limited and even dies grows in value and appreciation; it is the spiritual version of supply and demand. If we lived forever, they say, we would never take life seriously or learn to love what is. I think that is probably true. Being held long and hard inside limits and tension, incarnate moments—crucibles for sure—allows us to search for and often find "the reconciling third" or the unified field beneath it all. "The most personal becomes the most universal," Chardin loved to say.

Reality, creation, nature itself, what I call the "the First Body of Christ," has no choice in the matter of necessary suffering. It lives the message without saying yes or no to it. It holds and resolves all the foundational forces, all the elementary principles and particles within itself—willingly it seems. This is the universe in its wholeness, the "great nest of being," including even the powerless, invisible, and weak parts that have so little freedom or possibility. "The Second Body of Christ," the formal church, always has the freedom to say yes or no. That very freedom allows it to say no much of the time, especially to any talk of dying, stumbling, admitting mistakes, or falling. We see this rather clearly in the recent financial and sexual scandals of the church. Yet God seems ready and willing to wait for, and to empower, free will and a free "yes." Love only happens in the realm of freedom.

Yet I know that I avoid this daily dying too. The church has been for me a broad education and experience in passion, death, and resurrection by forcing me to go deep in one place. It, and the Franciscans, still offer me an accountability community for what I say I believe, which I find is necessary if I am to live with any long-term integrity. The Dalai Lama and Mother Teresa said the same. Over many years now, the practical church has given me the tools and the patience that allow me to try to fill what Parker Palmer calls "the tragic gap," as almost nothing else does. Both the church's practice and its Platonic pronouncements *create tragic gaps for any person with an operative head and a beating heart*. But remember, even a little bit of God is well worth loving, and even a little bit of truth and love goes a long way. The church has given me much more than a little bit. Like all limited parents, it has been a "good enough" church, and thus has taught me how to see that goodness everywhere, even in other limit situations, as Karl Jaspers called them. But in the end, "Only God is good," as Jesus said to the rich young man.

So the church is both my greatest intellectual and moral problem and my most consoling home. She is both pathetic whore and frequent bride. There is still a marvelous marriage with such a bride, and many whores do occasionally become brides too. In a certain but real sense, the church itself is the first cross that Jesus is crucified on, as we limit, mangle, and try to control the always too big message. All the churches seem to crucify Jesus again and again by their inability to receive his whole body, but they often resurrect him too. I am without doubt a microcosm of this universal church.

The church has never persecuted me or limited me in any way — quite the contrary, which is really quite amazing. Maybe that is the only reason I can talk this way, I hope without rancor or agenda. She has held me, and yet also held me at arm's length, which is more than enough holding. The formal church has always been a halfhearted bride for me, while the Franciscans have been considerably better. The Gospel itself is my full wedding partner. It always tells me the truth, and loves me *through things* till I arrive somewhere new and good and much more spacious.

So I offer this personal apologia for those of you who perhaps are wondering why I quote Jesus so much. You might be saying, "Does it really matter?" or "Does it have to be in the Bible to be true?" Well, I quote Jesus because I still consider him to be *the* spiritual authority of the Western world, whether we follow him or not. He is always spot-on at the deeper levels and when we understand him in his own explosive context. One does not even need to believe in his divinity to realize that Jesus is seeing at a much higher level than most of us.

For some of you, my quoting Jesus is the only way you will trust me; for others, it gives you more reasons to mistrust me, but I have to take both risks. If I dared to present all of these ideas simply as my ideas, or because they match modern psychology or old mythology, I would be dishonest. Jesus for me always clinches the deal, and I sometimes wonder why I did not listen to him in the first place.

Not surprisingly, many of the findings of modern psychology, anthropology, and organizational behavior give us new windows and vocabulary into Jesus' transcendent message. As you can see, I love to make use of these many tools. Let's look at one example of something that surely seems like entirely unnecessary suffering, which is said in a way that many people have not been prepared to hear if it were not for the findings of modern psychology and the behavioral sciences.

"HATING" FAMILY

In this heading, I am talking about those most problematic lines at the beginning of this chapter, in which Jesus talks about "leaving" or even "hating" mother, father, sister, brother, and family. Everything in us says that he surely cannot mean this, but if you are talking about moving into the second half of life, where we are about to go, he is in fact directing us correctly and courageously.

First of all, do you recognize that he is actually undoing the fourth commandment of Moses, which tells us to "honor your father and mother"? This commandment is necessary for the first half of life, and, one hopes, it can be possible forever. As we move into the second half of life, however, we are very often at odds with our natural family and the "dominant consciousness" of our cultures. It is true more often than I would have ever imagined. Many people are kept from mature religion because of the pious, immature, or rigid expectations of their first-half-of-life family. Even Jesus, whose family thought he was "crazy" (Mark 3:21), had to face this dilemma firsthand. The very fact that the evangelist would risk associating the word "crazy" with Jesus shows how Jesus was surely not following the expected and mainline script for his culture or his religion.

One of the major blocks against the second journey is what we would now call the "collective," the crowd, our society, or our extended family. Some call it the crab bucket syndrome—you try to get out, but the other crabs just keep pulling you back in. What passes for morality or spirituality in the vast majority of people's lives is *the way everybody they grew up with thinks.* Some would call it conditioning or even imprinting. Without very real inner work, most folks never move beyond it. You might get beyond it in a negative sense, by reacting or rebelling against it, but it is much less common to get out of the crab bucket in a positive way. That is what we want here. Jesus uses quite strong words to push us out of the family nest and to name a necessary suffering at the most personal, counterintuitive, and sentimental level possible.

It takes a huge push, much self-doubt, and some degree of separation for people to find their own soul and their own destiny apart from what Mom and Dad always wanted them to be and do. To move beyond family-of-origin stuff, local church stuff, cultural stuff, flag-and-country stuff is a path that few of us follow positively and with integrity. The pull is just too great, and the loyal soldier fills us with appropriate guilt, shame, and self-doubt, which, as we said earlier, feels like the very voice of God.

So Jesus pulls no punches, saying you *must "hate"* your home base in some way and make choices beyond it. I am happy he said this, or I would never have had the courage to believe how it might be true. It takes therapists years to achieve the same result and reestablish appropriate boundaries from wounding parents and early authority figures, and to heal the *inappropriate shame* in those who have been wounded. We all must leave home to find the real and larger home, which is so important that we will develop it more fully in the next chapter. The nuclear family has far too often been the enemy of the global family and mature spiritual seeking.

Perhaps it has never struck you how consistently the great religious teachers and founders leave home, go on pilgrimage to far-off places, do a major turnabout, choose downward mobility; and how often it is their parents, the established religion at that time, spiritual authorities, and often even civil authorities who fight against them. Read the biographies of Hindu sadhus, Buddha, Ashoka, Abraham, Joseph, Moses, Jesus, Sufi saints, Francis, Clare, and the numerous hermits and pilgrims of Cappadocia, Mt. Athos, and Russia. You will see that this pattern is rather universal.

Instead of our "Don't leave home without it" mentality, the spiritual greats' motto seems to be "Leave home to find it!" And of course, they were never primarily talking just about physical home, but about all the validations, securities, illusions, prejudices, smallness — and hurts too — that home and family always imply.

Of course, to be honest and consistent, one must ask if "church family" is not also a family that one has to eventually "hate" in this very same way, and with the same scandal involved as hating the natural family. (We will address this in a later chapter under the rubric of "emerging Christianity.")

I encourage you to reread the epigraphs at the beginning of this chapter. They are pretty strong, almost brutal, by contemporary standards; but they make very clear that there is a necessary suffering that cannot be avoided, which Jesus calls "losing our very life," or losing what I and others call the "false self." Your false self is your role, title, and personal image that is largely a creation of your own mind and attachments. *It will and must die in exact correlation to how much you want the Real.* "How much false self are you willing to shed to find your True Self?" is the lasting question.[2] Such necessary suffering will always feel like dying, which is what good spiritual teachers will tell you about very honestly. (Alcoholics Anonymous is notoriously successful here!) If your spiritual guides do not talk to you about dying, they are not good spiritual guides!

Your True Self is who you objectively are from the beginning, in the mind and heart of God, "the face you had before you were born," as the Zen masters say. It is your substantial self, your absolute identity, which can be neither gained nor lost by any technique, group affiliation, morality, or formula whatsoever. The surrendering of our false self, which we have usually taken for our absolute identity, yet is merely a relative identity, is the necessary suffering needed to find "the pearl of great price" that is always hidden inside this lovely but passing shell.

HOME AND HOMESICKNESS

Old men ought to be explorers
Here and there does not matter
We must be still and still moving
Into another intensity
For another union, a deeper communion
—T. S. ELIOT, "EAST COKER"

So now we move toward the goal, the very purpose of human life, "another intensity . . . a deeper communion," as Eliot calls it, that which the container is meant to hold, support, and foster. Not the fingers pointing to the moon, but the moon itself—and now including the dark side of the moon too. The fullness and inner freedom of the second half of life is what Homer seemed unable to describe. Perhaps he was not there himself yet, perhaps too young, yet he intuited its call and necessity. It was too "dark" for him perhaps, but he did point toward a further journey, and only then a truly final journey home. The goal in sacred story is always to come back home, after getting the protagonist to leave home in the first place! A contradiction? A paradox? Yes, but now home has a whole new meaning, never imagined before. As always, it *transcends but includes* one's initial experience of home.

The archetypal idea of "home" points in two directions at once. It points backward toward an original hint and taste for union, starting in the body of our mother. We all came from some kind of home, even a bad one, that always plants the foundational seed of a possible and ideal paradise. And it points forward, urging us toward the realization that this hint and taste of union might actually be true. It guides us like an inner compass or a "homing" device. In Homer's *Odyssey,* it is the same home, the island Ithaca, that is both the beginning and the end of the journey. Carl Jung, who so often says things concisely, offers this momentous insight: "Life is a luminous pause between two great mysteries, which themselves are one."[1] That is precisely what I want to say here.

Somehow the end is in the beginning, and the beginning points toward the end. We are told that even children with a sad or abusive childhood still long for "home" or "Mother" in some idealized form and still yearn to return to it somehow, maybe just to do it right this time. What is going on there? Agreeing with Jung, I believe that the One Great Mystery is revealed at the beginning and forever beckons us forward toward its full realization. Most of us cannot let go of this implanted promise. Some would call this homing device their soul, and some would call it the indwelling Holy Spirit, and some might just call it nostalgia or dreamtime. All I know is that it will not be ignored. It calls us both backward and forward, to our foundation and our future, at the same time. It also feels like grace from within us and at the same time beyond us. The soul lives in such eternally deep time. Wouldn't it make sense that God would plant in us a desire for what God already wants to give us? I am sure of it.

To understand better, let's look at the telling word *homesick*. This usually connotes something sad or nostalgic, an emptiness that looks either backward or forward for satisfaction. I am going to use it in an entirely different way, because now you are ready for it. I want to propose that we are both sent and drawn by the same Force, which is precisely what Christians mean when they say the Cosmic Christ is both alpha and omega. We are both driven and called forward by a kind of deep homesickness, it seems. There is an inherent and *desirous dissatisfaction* that both sends and draws us forward, and it comes from our original and radical union with God. What appears to be past and future is in fact the same home, the same call, and the same God, for whom "a thousand years are like a single day" (Psalm 90:4) and a single day like a thousand years.

In *The Odyssey,* the stirring of longing and dissatisfaction is symbolized by the collapse of Troy and the inability of most of the Greeks to return home. It seems they had forgotten about home, had made home in a foreign land, or were not that determined to return home (which are all excellent descriptions of the typical detours or dead ends on the spiritual journey!). Only Odysseus was trying to get home at all costs, and he is the stand-in for what we all must be. Those who do not seek their home are symbolized perhaps by the lotus eaters whom Odysseus encounters, who forgot themselves and lost their own depths and consciousness. It has been said that 90 percent of people seem to live 90 percent of their lives on cruise control, which is to be unconscious.

The Holy Spirit is that aspect of God that works largely from within and "secretly," at "the deepest levels of our desiring," as so many of the mystics have said. That's why the mystical tradition could only resort to subtle metaphors like wind, fire, descending doves, and flowing water to describe the Spirit. More than anything else, the Spirit keeps us connected and safely inside an already existing flow, if we but allow it. We never "create" or earn the Spirit; we discover this inner abiding as we learn to draw upon our deepest inner life. This utterly unified field is always *given,* as Annie Dillard said.

I think also of Hermann Hesse's *Steppenwolf,* in which he says, "We have no one to guide us. Our only guide is our homesickness." Even Dorothy is guided forward to Oz and back to Kansas by her constant love and search for home. It is part of the reason the story has such lasting appeal. On the level of soul, I believe these sources are all correct. Home is another word for the Spirit that we are, our True

Self in God. *The self same moment that we find God in ourselves, we also find ourselves inside God,* and this is the full homecoming, according to Teresa of Avila. Until then we are homesick, although today most would probably just call it loneliness, isolation, longing, sadness, restlessness, or even a kind of depression.

The common word for this inner abiding place of the Spirit, which is also a place of longing, has usually been the word *soul.* We have our soul already — we do not "get" it by any purification process or by joining any group or from the hands of a bishop. The end is already planted in us at the beginning, and it gnaws away at us until we get there freely and consciously. The most a bishop or sacrament can do is to "fan [this awareness] into flame" (2 Timothy 1:6), and sometimes it does. But sometimes great love and great suffering are even bigger fans for this much-needed flame.

The good news is that there *is* a guide, a kind of medical advocate, an inner compass — and it resides within each of us. "Included inside the box," as the ads always say. As the Scriptures put it, "The love of God has been poured into our hearts through the Holy Spirit that has been given to us" (Romans 5:5). In another place we are promised, "You will not be left orphaned" (John 14:18) without a mother or home. This is probably one of the many reasons the Holy Spirit was usually considered feminine.

This Holy Spirit guiding all of us from home and toward home is also described in John's Gospel as an "advocate" ("a defense attorney," as *paraclete* literally means, John 14:16), who will "teach us" and "remind us," as if some part of us already knew but still needed an inner buzz or alarm clock to wake us up. The Holy Spirit is always entirely *for us*, more than we are for ourselves, it seems. She speaks in our favor against the negative voices that judge and condemn us. This gives us all such hope—now we do not have to do life all by ourselves, or even do life perfectly "right." Our life will be "done unto us," just as happened to Mary (Luke 1:38). Although on another level we are doing it too. Both are equally true.

This mystery has been called the *conspiracy* ("co-breathing") of God, and is still one of the most profound ways to understand what is happening between God and the soul. True spirituality is always a deep "co-operating" (Romans 8:28) between two. True spirituality is a kind of *synergy* in which both parties give and both parties receive to create one shared truth and joy.[2]

The ancients rightly called this internal longing for wholeness "fate" or "destiny," the "inner voice" or the "call of the gods." It has an inevitability, authority, and finality to it, and was at the heart of almost all mythology. Almost all heroes heard an inner voice that spoke to them. In fact, their heroism was in their ability to hear that voice and to risk following it—wherever! Sadly, such inner comfort is the very thing we lack today at almost all levels. Our problem now is that we seriously doubt that there is any vital reality to the spiritual world, so we hear no life-changing voices—true even for many who go to church, temple, or mosque.

For postmodern people, the universe is not inherently enchanted, as it was for the ancients. We have to do all the "enchanting" ourselves. This leaves us alone, confused, and doubtful. There is no meaning already in place for our discovery and enjoyment. We have to create all meaning by ourselves in such an inert and empty world, and most of us do not seem to succeed very well. This is the burden of living in our heady and lonely time, when we think it is all up to us.

The gift of living in our time, however, is that we are more and more discovering that the sciences, particularly physics, astrophysics, anthropology, and biology, are confirming many of the deep intuitions of religion, and at a rather quick pace in recent years. The universe really is "inspirited matter," we now know, and is not merely inert. Now we might call it instinct, evolution, nuclear fusion, DNA, hardwiring, the motherboard, healing, growth, or just springtime, but nature clearly continues to renew itself from within. *God seems to have created things that continue to create and recreate themselves from the inside out*. It is no longer God's one-time creation *or* evolution; rather, God's form of creation precisely *is* evolution. *Finally God is allowed to be fully incarnate, which was supposed to be Christianity's big trump card from the beginning!* It has taken us a long time to get here, and dualistic thinkers still cannot jump the hurdle.

Remember Odysseus's oar that an inland wayfarer saw as a winnowing fan? His oar (or occupation) had become a tool for inner work, a means for knowing the difference between the wheat and chaff, essentials and nonessentials, which is precisely the turn toward discernment and subtlety that we come to in the second half of life. What a strange but brilliant symbol Homer offers us. No surprise that this marks the end of Odysseus's journey! Now he can *go home* because he has, in fact, *come home* to his true and full self. His sailing and oaring days of mere "outer performance" are over, and he can now rest in the simplicity and ground of his own deeper life. He is free to stop his human *doing* and can at last enjoy his human *being*.

Because important things bear repeating in different forms, let me summarize the direction of my thought here. I am saying that

- We are created with an *inner drive and necessity* that sends all of us looking for our True Self, whether we know it or not. This journey is a spiral and never a straight line.
- We are created with an inner restlessness and call that urges us on to the risks and promises of *a second half to our life*. There is a God-size hole in all of us, waiting

to be filled. God creates the very dissatisfaction that only grace and finally divine love can satisfy.

- We dare not try to fill our souls and minds with numbing addictions, diversionary tactics, or mindless distractions. The shape of evil is much more *superficiality* and blindness than the usually listed "hot sins." God hides, and is found, precisely in the *depths* of everything, even and maybe especially in the deep fathoming of our fallings and failures. Sin is to stay on the *surface* of even holy things, like Bible, sacrament, or church.

- If we go to the depths of anything, we will begin to knock upon something substantial, "real," and with a timeless quality to it. We will move from the starter kit of "belief" to an actual inner *knowing*. This is most especially true if we have ever (1) loved deeply, (2) accompanied someone through the mystery of dying, (3) or stood in genuine life-changing *awe* before mystery, time, or beauty.

- This "something real" is what all the world religions were pointing to when they spoke of heaven, nirvana, bliss, or enlightenment. They were not wrong at all; their only mistake was that they pushed it off into the next world. *If heaven is later, it is because it is first of all now.*

- These events become the pledge, guarantee, hint, and promise of an eternal something. Once you touch upon the Real, there is an inner insistence that the Real, if it is the Real, has to be forever. Call it wishful thinking, if you will, but this insistence has been a constant intuition since the beginnings of humanity. Jesus made it into a promise, as when he tells the Samaritan woman that "the spring within her will well up unto eternal life" (John 4:14). In other words, heaven/union/love now emerge from within us, much more than from a mere belief system or any belonging system, which largely remains on the outside of the self.

And so, like Odysseus, we leave from Ithaca and we come back to Ithaca, but now it is fully home, because all is included, and nothing wasted or hated; even the dark parts are used in our favor. All is forgiven. What else could home-coming be?! A lesser-known Egyptian poet, C. P. Cavafy, expresses this understanding most beautifully, in a famous poem called "Ithaca," which has many translations, though this is largely my own:

Ithaca has now given you the beautiful voyage.
Without her, you would never have taken the road,
With the great wisdom you have gained on your voyage,
With so much of your own experience now,
You must finally know what Ithaca really means.

AMNESIA AND THE BIG PICTURE

 God wanted to give human beings their full-ness right from the beginning, but they were incapable of receiving it, because they were still little children.

—ST. IRENAEUS (125–203 A.D.), "AGAINST HERESIES"

 It is the whole of nature, extending from the beginning to the end that constitutes the one image of God Who Is.

—ST. GREGORY OF NYSSA (330–395 A.D.), "ON THE CREATION OF MAN"

As many others have said in different ways, we all seem to suffer from a tragic case of mistaken identity. Life is a matter of becoming fully and consciously who we already are, but it is a self that we largely do not know. It is as though we are all suffering from a giant case of amnesia. As mentioned before, the protagonists in so many fairy tales are already nobles, royal, daughters and sons of the king or even the gods. But their identity is hidden from them, and the story line pivots around this discovery.

They have to grow up to fathom their own identity. That fathoming is the very purpose of the journey.

It is religion's job to teach us and guide us on this discovery of our True Self, but it usually makes the mistake of turning this into a worthiness contest of some sort, a private performance, or some kind of religious achievement on our part, through our belonging to the right group, practicing the right rituals, or believing the right things. These are just tugboats to get you away from the shore and out into the right sea; they are the oars to get you working and engaged with the Mystery. But never confuse these instruments with your profound "ability to share in the divine nature" itself (2 Peter 1:4). It is the common, and in this case tragic, confusion of the medium with the message, or the style with the substance.

It was largely the fathers of the early church, and especially the Eastern Church, who never compromised on what they called *theosis* or "divinization," as we see in the powerful quotes above. There are many more such astounding quotes,[1] but this very memory is also a part of Western amnesia. The Gospel was just too good to be true—for a future-oriented, product-oriented, and win-lose worldview.

Such deep knowing about our true selves is surely what John is pointing to when he says, "It is not because you do not know the truth that I am writing to you, but rather *because you know it already*!" (1 John 2:21). Otherwise he would not have had the self-confidence to write about spiritual things with such authority, nor would I. We are all drawing upon a Larger Source, the unified field, the shared Spirit. I am also relying upon your inner, deep-time *recognition* more than any linear *cognition*. Maybe you have noticed that by now. I hope so. The English poet Wordsworth put it so beautifully:

> Our birth is but a sleep and a forgetting:
> The Soul that rises with us, our Life's Star
> Hath had elsewhere its setting,
> And cometh from afar:
> Not in entire forgetfulness.
> And not in utter nakedness,
> But trailing clouds of glory do we come
> From God, who is our home:
> Heaven lies about us in our infancy!
> Shades of the prison-house begin to close
> upon the growing boy,
> But he beholds the light, and whence it flows,
> He sees it in his joy.[2]

That bit of his larger poem should be enough to make Wordsworth an honorary doctor of the church! Mature religion is always trying to get you out of the closing prison-house of the false self. Many have said before me that spirituality is much more about unlearning than learning,

because the "growing boy" is usually growing into major
illusions, all of which must be undone to free him from
prison and take him back to his beginnings in God. "Unless
you change, and become like a little child, you will not
enter the kingdom of God," Jesus says (Matthew 18:3).
And he says this in response to the egotistic and ambitious
question of the apostles, who were asking him, "Who is
the greatest?"

I have sometimes wondered if we might be surprised
and disappointed by what it means that our faith is "built
on the faith of the apostles," as we have so proudly sung
and proclaimed. They barely ever got the point, and seem
as thoroughly foolish as we are; but God still used them,
because like all of us they were little children too. I indeed
share in this very faith. We are all and forever beginners in
the journey toward God and truth.

"HEAVEN" AND "HELL"

Any discovery or recovery of our divine union has been
called "heaven" by most traditions. Its loss has been called
"hell." The tragic result of our amnesia is that we cannot
imagine that these terms are first of all referring to present
experiences. *When you do not know who you are, you
push all enlightenment off into a possible future reward
and punishment system, within which hardly anyone wins.*
Only the True Self knows that heaven is now and that its

loss is hell—now. The false self makes religion into the old "evacuation plan for the next world," as my friend Brian McLaren puts it. Amnesia has dire consequences. No wonder the Jews say "remember" so much.

A person who has found his or her True Self has learned how to live in the big picture, as a part of deep time and all of history. This change of frame and venue is called living in "the kingdom of God" by Jesus, and it is indeed a major about-face. This necessitates, of course, that we let go of our own smaller kingdoms, which we normally do not care to do. Life is all about *practicing for heaven*. We practice by choosing union freely—ahead of time—and now. Heaven is the state of union both here and later. *As now, so will it be then*. No one is in heaven unless he or she wants to be, and all are in heaven as soon as they live in union. Everyone is in heaven when he or she has plenty of room for communion and no need for exclusion. The more room you have to include, the bigger your heaven will be.

Perhaps this is what Jesus means by there being "many rooms in my Father's house" (John 14:2). If you go to heaven alone, wrapped in your private worthiness, it is by definition *not* heaven. If your notion of heaven is based on exclusion of anybody else, then it is by definition *not* heaven. The more you exclude, the more hellish and lonely your existence always is. How could anyone enjoy the "perfect happiness" of any heaven if she knew her loved ones were not there, or were being tortured for all eternity?

It would be impossible. Remember our Christian prayer, "on earth as it is heaven." As now, so then; as here, so there. We will all get exactly what we want and ask for. You can't beat that.

If you accept a punitive notion of God, who punishes or even eternally tortures those who do not love him, then you have an absurd universe where most people on this earth end up being more loving than God! God excludes no one from union, but must allow us to exclude ourselves in order for us to maintain our freedom. Our word for that exclusion is hell, and it must be maintained as a logical possibility. There must be the logical possibility of excluding oneself from union and to choose separation or superiority over community and love. No one is in hell unless that individual himself or herself chooses a final aloneness and separation. It is all about *desire*, both allowing and drawing from the deepest level of our desiring. It is interesting to me that the official church has never declared a single person to be in hell, not even Judas, Hitler, or Stalin.

Jesus touched and healed anybody who desired it and asked for it, and there were no other prerequisites for his healings. Check it out yourself. Why would Jesus' love be so unconditional while he was in this world, and suddenly become totally conditional after death? Is it the same Jesus? Or does Jesus change his policy after his resurrection? The belief in heaven and hell is meant to maintain freedom on all sides, with God being the most free of all, to forgive and include, to heal and to bless even God's seeming "enemies." How could Jesus ask us to bless, forgive, and heal our enemies, which he clearly does (Matthew 5:43–48), unless God is doing it first and always? Jesus told us to love our enemies because he saw his Father doing it all the time, and all spirituality is merely the "imitation of God" (Ephesians 5:1).

Ken Wilber described the later stages of life well when he said that *the classic spiritual journey always begins elitist and ends egalitarian. Always!* We see it in Judaism, starting with the Jews' early elite chosenness and ending in prophets without borders, in the heady new sect of Christianity that soon calls itself "catholic" or universal. We see it in Sufi Islam and Hindu Krishna consciousness, which sees God's joy everywhere. We see it in mystics like William Blake or Lady Julian, who start with a grain of sand or a hazelnut and soon find themselves swimming in infinity. We see it in the Native American sweat lodge, where the participant ends by touching his sweaty body to the earth and saying "All my relations!" I wish we could expect as much from Catholics when they so frequently "go to communion."

Life moves first toward diversity and then toward union of that very diversity at ever higher levels. It is the old philosophical problem of "the one and the many," which Christianity should have resolved in its belief in God as Trinity. *Up to now we have been more in love with elitism than with any egalitarianism; we liked being the "one," but just did not know how to include the many in that very One.*

Even Pope John Paul II said that heaven and hell were primarily eternal states of consciousness more than geographical places of later reward and punishment.[3] We seem to be our own worst enemies, and *we forget or deny things that are just too good to be true.* The ego clearly prefers an economy of merit, where we can divide the world into winners and losers, to any economy of grace, where merit or worthiness loses all meaning.[4] In the first case, at least a few of us good guys attain glory. In the second case, all the glory is to God.

The healing of your amnesia, and any entry into heaven, is the rediscovery of the still-enchanted world of a happy child, but it now includes the maturing experiences of love, unique life journeys, all your relations, and just enough failures to keep you honest and grounded. This "second childhood" perhaps needs a personal or practical example, so allow me to talk about a bit of my own experience in the second half of my own life.

CHAPTER 9

A SECOND SIMPLICITY

Beyond rational and critical thinking, we need to be called again. This can lead to the discovery of a "second naiveté," which is a return to the joy of our first naiveté, but now totally new, inclusive, and mature thinking.

—PAUL RICOEUR

People are so afraid of being considered pre-rational that they avoid and deny the very possibility of the transrational. Others substitute mere pre-rational emotions for authentic religious experience, which is always transrational.

—KEN WILBER

These quick summaries (not precise quotations) are from two great thinkers who more or less describe for me what happened on my own spiritual and intellectual journey. I began as a very conservative pre–Vatican II Roman Catholic, living in innocent Kansas, pious and law abiding, buffered and bounded by my parents' stable marriage and many lovely liturgical traditions that sanctified my time and space. That was my first wonderful simplicity. I was a very happy child and young man, and all who knew me then would agree.

Yet I grew in my experience, and was gradually educated in a much larger world of the 1960s and 1970s, with degrees in philosophy and theology, and a broad liberal arts education given me by the Franciscans. That education was a second journey into rational complexity. I left the garden, just as Adam and Eve had to do, even though my new Scripture awareness made it obvious that Adam and Eve were probably not historical figures, but important archetypal symbols. Darn it! My parents back in Kansas were worried! I was heady with knowledge and "enlightenment" and was surely not in Kansas anymore. I had passed, like Dorothy, "over the rainbow." It is sad and disconcerting for a while, outside the garden, and some lovely innocence dies, yet "angels with flaming swords prevented my return" to the first garden (Genesis 3:24). There was no going back, unfortunately. Life was much easier on the childhood side of the rainbow.

As time passed, I became simultaneously very traditional and very progressive, and I have probably continued to be so to this day. I found a much larger and even happier garden (note the new garden described at the end of the Bible in Revelation 21!). I totally believe in Adam and Eve now, but on about ten more levels. (*Literalism is usually the lowest and least level of meaning.*) I have lived much of my subsequent life like a man without a country—and yet a man who could go to any country and be at home. This nowhere land surprised even me. I no longer fit in with either the mere liberals or the mere conservatives. This was my first strong introduction to paradox, and it took most of midlife to figure out what had happened—and how—and why it *had* to happen.

This "pilgrim's progress" was, for me, sequential, natural, and organic as the circles widened. I was lucky enough to puddle-jump between countries, cultures, and concepts because of my public speaking; yet the solid ground of the perennial tradition never really shifted. It was only the lens, the criteria, the inner space, and the scope that continued to expand. I was always being moved toward greater differentiation and larger viewpoints, and simultaneously toward a greater inclusivity in my ideas, a deeper understanding of people, and a more honest sense of justice. God always became bigger and led me to bigger places. If God could "include" and allow, then why not I? I did not see many examples of God "smiting" his enemies; in fact, it was usually God's friends who got smited, as Teresa of Avila noted! If God asked me to love unconditionally and universally, then it was clear that God operated in the same way.

Soon there was a much bigger world than the United States and the Roman Catholic Church, which I eventually realized were also paradoxes. The *e pluribus unum* ("out of many, one") on American coinage did not include very "many" of its own people (blacks, gays, Native Americans, poor folks, and so on), and as a Christian I finally had to be either Roman or catholic, and I continue to choose the catholic end of that spectrum. Either Jesus is the "savior of the world" (John 4:42), or he is not much of a savior at all. Either America treats the rest of the world democratically, or it does not really believe in democracy at all. That is the way I see it.

But this slow process of transformation and the realizations that came with it were not either-or decisions; they were great big *both-and realizations*. None of it happened without much prayer, self-doubt, study, and conversation, but the journey itself led me to a deepening sense of what the church calls holiness, what Americans call freedom, and what psychology calls wholeness. I could transcend now precisely because I was able to include and broaden. *Paul Ricoeur's first naiveté was the best way to begin the journey, and a second naiveté was the easiest way to continue that same journey*, without becoming angry, split, alienated, or ignorant. I now hope and believe that a kind of second simplicity is the very goal of mature adulthood and mature religion. Although we often used it in a derogatory way, I wonder if this was not our intuition when we spoke of older people as in a "second childhood"? Maybe that is where we are supposed to go? Maybe that is what several poets meant when they said "the child is father of the man"?

My small personal viewpoint as a central reference point for anything, or for rightly judging anything, gradually faded as life went on. The very meaning of the word *universe* is to "turn around one thing." I know *I* am not that one thing. There is either some Big Truth in this universe, or there is no truth that is always reliable; there is we hope, some pattern behind it all (even if the pattern is exception!), or it begins to be a very incoherent universe, which is what many postmodern people seem to have accepted. I just can't.

Mature religions, and now some scientists, say that we are hardwired for the Big Picture, for transcendence, for ongoing growth, for union with ourselves and everything else.[1] Either God is for everybody and the divine DNA is somehow in all of the creatures, or this God is not God by any common definition, or even much of a god at all. We are driven, kicking and screaming, toward ever higher levels of union and ability to include (to forgive others for being "other"), it seems to me. "Everything that rises must converge," as Teilhard de Chardin put it.

But many get stopped and fixated at lower levels where God seems to torture and exclude forever those people who don't agree with "him" or get "his" name right. *How could you possibly feel safe, free, loved, trustful, or invited by such a small God?* Jesus undid this silliness himself when he said, "You, evil as you are, know how to give good things to your children. . . . If you, then how much more, God!" (Matthew 7:11). The God I have met and been loved by in my life journey is always an experience of "how much more!" If we are created in the image and likeness of God, then whatever good, true, or beautiful things we can say about humanity or creation we can say of God exponentially. God is the beauty of creation and humanity multiplied to the infinite power.

ANXIETY AND DOUBT

For me, this wondrous universe cannot be an incoherent and accidental cosmos, nor can it be grounded in evil, although I admit that this intellectual leap and bias toward beauty is still an act of faith and trust on my part. Yet this act of faith has also been the common sense and intuition of 99 percent of the people who have ever lived. I further believe that a free and loving God would create things that continue to recreate themselves, exactly as all parents desire for their children. God seems to want *us* to be in on the deal! The Great Work is ours too.

I do, however, hold a certain degree of doubt about the how, if, when, where, and who of it all. Creative doubt keeps me with a perpetual "beginner's mind," which is a wonderful way to keep growing, keep humble, and keep living in happy wonder. Yet it is this very *quiet inner unfolding of things* that seems to create the most doubt and anxiety for many believers. They seem to prefer a "touch of the magic wand" kind of God (Tinker Bell?) to a God who works secretly and humbly, and who includes *us* in on the process and the conclusion. This is the only way I can understand why a Christian would think evolution is any kind of faith problem whatsoever. The only price we pay for living in the Big Picture is to hold a bit of doubt and anxiety about the exact how, if, when, where, and who of it all, but never the *that*. Unfortunately, most Christians are not well trained in holding opposites for very long, or living with what could be very creative tension.

Basic religious belief is a vote for some *coherence, purpose, benevolence, and direction in the universe*, and I suspect it emerges from all that we said in the last chapter about home, soul, and the homing device of Spirit. This belief is perhaps the same act of faith as that of Albert Einstein, who said before he discovered his unified field that he assumed just two things: that whatever reality is, it would show itself to be both "simple and beautiful." I agree! *Faith in any religion is always somehow saying that God is one and God is good, and if so, then all of reality must be that simple and beautiful too*. The Jewish people made it their creed, wrote it on their hearts, and inscribed it on their doorways (Deuteronomy 6:4–5), so that they could not and would not forget it.

I worry about "true believers" who cannot carry any doubt or anxiety at all, as Thomas the Apostle and Mother Teresa learned to do. People who are so certain always seem like Hamlet's queen "protesting too much" and trying too hard. *To hold the full mystery of life is always to endure its other half*, which is the equal mystery of death and doubt. To know anything fully is always to hold that part of it which is still mysterious and unknowable.

After almost seventy years, I am still a mystery to myself! Our youthful demand for certainty does eliminate most anxiety on the conscious level, so I can see why many of us stay in such a control tower during the first half of life. *We do not have enough experience of wholeness to include all of its parts yet.* First-half-of-life "naiveté" includes a kind of excitement and happiness that is hard to let go of, unless you know there is an even deeper and tested kind of happiness out ahead of you. But you do not know that yet in the early years! Which is why those in the second half of life must tell you about it! Without elders, a society perishes socially and spiritually.

First naiveté is the earnest and dangerous innocence we sometimes admire in young zealots, but it is also the reason we do not follow them if we are smart, and why we should not elect them or follow them as leaders. It is probably necessary to eliminate most doubt when you are young; doing so is a good survival technique. *But such worldviews are not true—and they are not wisdom.* Wisdom happily lives with mystery, doubt, and "unknowing," and in such living, ironically resolves that very mystery to some degree. I have never figured out why unknowing becomes another kind of knowing, but it surely seems to be.[2] It takes a lot of learning to finally "learn ignorance" (*docta ignorantia*) as

Dionysius, Augustine, Bonaventure, and Nicholas of Cusa all agreed.

I must sadly admit that I am impatient with people who do not see things this way; but it took me a long time to get here myself, so I have learned to be more patient and compassionate over time. I don't need to push the river as much now, or own the river, or get everybody in my precise river; nor do others have to name the river the same way I do in order for me to trust them or their goodwill. It takes lots of drowning in your own too tiny river to get to this big and good place.

I, like everyone else, have had my many experiences, teachings, and teachers, but as T. S. Eliot puts it in the *Four Quartets,*

> We had the experience but missed the meaning,
> And approach to the meaning restores the experience
> In a different form, beyond any meaning
> We can assign to happiness.[3]

I know that Eliot's wording is dense, but it might be worth reading again. In the second half of life, we are not demanding our American constitutional right to the pursuit of happiness or that people must have our same experiences; rather, *simple meaning now suffices, and that becomes in itself a much deeper happiness.* As the body cannot live without food, so the soul cannot live without meaning.

Victor Frankl described this so well when he pointed out that some level of meaning was the only thing that kept people from total despair and suicide during the Holocaust. Humans are creators of meaning, and finding deep meaning in our experiences is not just another name for spirituality but is also the very shape of human happiness.

This new coherence, a unified field inclusive of the paradoxes, is precisely what gradually characterizes a second-half-of-life person. It feels like a return to simplicity after having learned from all the complexity. Finally, at last, one has lived long enough to see that "everything belongs,"[4] even the sad, absurd, and futile parts.

In the second half of life, we can give our energy to making even the painful parts and the formally excluded parts belong to the now unified field — especially people who are different, and those who have never had a chance. If you have forgiven yourself for being imperfect and falling, you can now do it for just about everybody else. If you have *not* done it for yourself, I am afraid you will likely pass on your sadness, absurdity, judgment, and futility to others. This is the tragic path of the many elderly people who have not become actual elders, probably because they were never eldered or mentored themselves.

Such people seem to have missed out on the joy and clarity of the first simplicity, perhaps avoided the interim complexity, and finally lost the great freedom and magnanimity of the second simplicity as well. We need to hold together all of the stages of life, and for some strange, wonderful reason, it all becomes quite "simple" as we approach our later years.

In fact, if this book is not making it very simple for you, I am doing it wrong or you are hearing it wrong. The great irony is that you must go through a necessary complexity (perhaps another word for necessary suffering) to return to any second simplicity. There is no nonstop flight from first to second naiveté.

CHAPTER 10

A BRIGHT SADNESS

I die by brightness and the Holy Spirit.
—THOMAS MERTON, "THE BLESSED VIRGIN
MARY COMPARED TO A WINDOW"

There is a gravitas in the second half of life, but it is now held up by a much deeper lightness, or "okayness." Our mature years are characterized by a kind of bright sadness and a sober happiness, if that makes any sense. I am just grabbing for words to describe many wonderful older people I have met. If you have met them, you know for yourself, and will find your own words. There is still darkness in the second half of life—in fact maybe even more. But there is now a changed capacity to hold it creatively and with less anxiety.

It is what John of the Cross called "luminous darkness," and it explains the simultaneous coexistence of deep suffering and intense joy in the saints, which would be impossible for most of us to even imagine. Eastern Orthodoxy believed that if something was authentic religious art, it would always have a bright sadness to it. I think I agree with them, and am saying the same of life itself.

117

In this second half of life, one has less and less need or interest in eliminating the negative or fearful, making again those old rash judgments, holding on to old hurts, or feeling any need to punish other people. Your superiority complexes have gradually departed in all directions. You do not fight these things anymore; they have just shown themselves too many times to be useless, ego based, counterproductive, and often entirely wrong. You learn to positively ignore and withdraw your energy from evil or stupid things rather than fight them directly.

You fight things only when you are directly called and equipped to do so. We all become a well-disguised mirror image of anything that we fight too long or too directly. That which we oppose determines the energy and frames the questions after a while. You lose all your inner freedom.

By the second half of life, you have learned ever so slowly, and with much resistance, that most frontal attacks on evil just produce another kind of evil in yourself, along with a very inflated self-image to boot, and incites a lot of push-back from those you have attacked. This seems to be one of the last lessons to be learned. Think of the cold Grand Inquisitor in *The Brothers Karamazov,* or the monk who tries to eliminate all humor in *The Name of the Rose,* or the frowning Koran burners of Florida. Holier-than-thou people usually end up holier than nobody.

Daily life now requires prayer and discernment more than knee-jerk responses toward either the conservative or liberal end of the spectrum. You have *a spectrum of responses* now, and they are not all predictable, as is too often the case with most knee-jerk responses. Law is still necessary, of course, but it is not your guiding star, or even close. It has been wrong and cruel too many times.

The Eight Beatitudes speak to you much more than the Ten Commandments now. I have always wondered why people never want to put a stone monument of the Eight Beatitudes on the courthouse lawn. Then I realize that the Eight Beatitudes of Jesus would probably not be very good for any war, any macho worldview, the wealthy, or our consumer economy. Courthouses are good and necessary first-half-of-life institutions. In the second half, you try instead to influence events, work for change, quietly persuade, change your own attitude, pray, or forgive instead of taking things to court.

Life is much more spacious now, the boundaries of the container having been enlarged by the constant addition of new experiences and relationships. You are like an expandable suitcase, and you became so almost without your noticing. Now you are just *here*, and here holds more than enough. Such "hereness," however, has its own heft, authority, and influence. Just watch true elders sitting in any circle of conversation; they are often defining the center, depth, and circumference of the dialogue just by being there! Most participants do not even know it is happening. When elders speak, they need very few words to make their point. Too many words, the use of which I am surely guilty, are not needed by true elders. Second simplicity has its own kind of brightness and clarity, but much of it is expressed in nonverbal terms, and only when really needed. If you talk too much or too loud, you are usually not an elder.

If we know anything at this stage, we know that we are all in this together and that we are all equally naked underneath our clothes. Which probably does not feel like a whole lot of knowing, but even this little bit of honesty gives us a strange and restful consolation. When you are young, you define yourself by differentiating yourself; now you look for the things we all share in common. You find happiness in alikeness, which has become much more obvious to you now; and you do not need to dwell on the differences between people or exaggerate the problems. Creating dramas has become boring.

In the second half of life, it is good just to be a part of the general dance. We do not have to stand out, make defining moves, or be better than anyone else on the dance floor. Life is more *participatory* than assertive, and there is no need for strong or further self-definition. God has taken care of all that, much better than we ever expected. The brightness comes from within now, and it is usually more than enough. The dance has a seriousness to it, but also an unself-conscious freedom of form that makes it bright and shining. Think of two old lovers quietly dancing to a soft clarinet and piano melody of the 1940s, safe and relaxed in one another's arms, and unconcerned whether anyone is watching. The dance is completely for its own sake.

At this stage, I no longer have to prove that I or my group is the best, that my ethnicity is superior, that my religion is the only one that God loves, or that my role and place in society deserve superior treatment. I am not preoccupied with collecting more goods and services; quite simply, my desire and effort—every day—is to pay back, to give back to the world a bit of what I have received. I now realize that I have been gratuitously given *to*—from the universe, from society, and from God. I try now, as Elizabeth Seton said, to "live simply so that others can simply live."

Erik Erikson calls someone at this stage a "generative" person, one who is eager and able to generate life from his or her own abundance and for the benefit of following generations. Because such people have built a good container, they are able to "contain" more and more truth, more and more neighbors, more and broader vision, more and more of a mysterious and outpouring God.

Their God is no longer small, punitive, or tribal. They once worshiped their raft; now they love the shore where it has taken them. They once defended signposts; now they have arrived where the signs pointed. They now enjoy the moon itself instead of fighting over whose finger points to it most accurately, quickly, or definitively.

One's growing sense of infinity and spaciousness is no longer found just "out there" but most especially "in here."

The inner and the outer have become one. You can trust your inner experience now, because even God has allowed it, used it, received it, and refined it. As St. Augustine dramatically put it in his *Confessions,*

> You were within, but I was without. You were with me, but I was not with you. So you called, you shouted, you broke through my deafness, you flared, blazed, and banished my blindness, you lavished your fragrance, and I gasped.[1]

It takes such gasping several times in your life to eventually rest in a bright sadness: you are sad because you now hold the pain of the larger world, and you wish everyone enjoyed what you now enjoy; but there is brightness because life is somehow—on some levels—still "very good," just as Genesis promised. Merton again says this best, as he concludes my favorite book of his: "It does not matter much [now], because no despair of ours can alter the reality of things, or stain the joy of the cosmic dance which is always there. . . . We are [now] invited to forget ourselves on purpose, cast our awful solemnity to the winds and join in the general dance."[2]

In the second half of life, we do not have strong and final opinions about everything, every event, or most people, as much as we allow things and people to delight us, sadden us, and truly influence us. We no longer need to change or adjust other people to be happy ourselves. Ironically, we are more than ever before in a position to change people — but we do not *need to* — and that makes all the difference. We have moved from doing to being to an utterly new kind of doing that flows almost organically, quietly, and by osmosis. Our actions are less compulsive. We do what we are called to do, and then try to let go of the consequences. We usually cannot do that very well when we are young.

This is human life in its crowning, and all else has been preparation and prelude for creating such a human work of art. Now we aid and influence other people simply by being who we are. Human integrity probably influences and moves people from potency to action more than anything else. It always deeply saddens me when old folks are still full of themselves and their absolute opinions about everything. Somehow they have not taken their needed place in the social fabric. We need their deep and studied passion so much more than their superficial and loudly stated principles. We need their peace more than their anger.

Yes, the second half of life is a certain kind of weight to carry, but no other way of being makes sense or gives you the deep satisfaction your soul now demands and even enjoys. This new and deeper passion is what people mean when they say, "I must do this particular thing or my life will not make sense" or "It is no longer a choice." Your life and your delivery system are now one, whereas before, your life and your occupation seemed like two different things. Your concern is not so much *to have what you love* anymore, but *to love what you have*—right now. This is a monumental change from the first half of life, so much so that it is almost the litmus test of whether you are in the second half of life at all.

The rules are all different now, and we often see it in older folks' freedom to give things away. Hoarding, possessing, collecting, and impressing others with their things, their house, or their travels are of less and less interest to them. Inner brightness, still holding life's sadness and joy, is its own reward, its own satisfaction, and their best and truest gift to the world. Such elders are the "grand" parents of the world. Children and other adults feel so safe and loved around them, and they themselves feel so needed and helpful to children, teens, and midlife adults. And they are! They are in their natural flow.

Strangely, all of life's problems, dilemmas, and diffi- culties are now resolved not by negativity, attack, criticism, force, or logical resolution, but always by falling into a larger "brightness." Hopkins called it "the dearest fresh- ness deep down things." This is the falling upward that we have been waiting for! One of the guiding principles of our Center for Action and Contemplation puts it this way: "The best criticism of the bad is the practice of the better." I learned this from my father St. Francis, who did not concentrate on attacking evil or others, but just spent his life *falling,* and falling many times into the good, the true, and the beautiful. It was the only way he knew how to fall into God.

Such inner brightness ends up being a much better and longer-lasting alternative to evil than any war, anger, violence, or ideology could ever be. All you have to do is meet one such shining person and you know that he or she is surely the goal of humanity and the delight of God. I hope you are becoming that shining person yourself, and that this book is helping you see it, allow it, and trust it. Otherwise, this book too will be just some more words—instead of words becoming flesh. Until it becomes flesh, it cannot shine and shine brightly.

CHAPTER 11

THE SHADOWLANDS

A light shines on in the darkness, a light that darkness cannot overcome.
—PROLOGUE TO JOHN'S GOSPEL 1:5

Make friends with your opponent quickly while he is taking you to court; or he will hand you over to the judge, and the judge to the officer, and the officer will throw you into prison. You will not get out until you have paid the last penny.
—MATTHEW 5:25–26

Despite the joys of such "brightness," we must also talk more about the paradoxical journey of getting there. By the second half of life, you have been in regular unwelcome contact with your shadow self, which gradually detaches you from your not-so-bright *persona* (meaning "stage mask" in Greek) that you so diligently constructed in the first half of life. Your stage mask is not bad, evil, or necessarily egocentric; it is just not "true." It is manufactured and sustained unconsciously by your mind; but it can and will die, as all fictions must die.

Persona and shadow are correlative terms. *Your shadow is what you refuse to see about yourself, and what you do not want others to see.* The more you have cultivated and protected a chosen persona, the more shadow work you will need to do. Be especially careful therefore of any idealized role or self-image, like that of minister, mother, doctor, nice person, professor, moral believer, or president of this or that. These are huge personas to live up to, and they trap many people in lifelong delusion. The more you are attached to and unaware of such a protected self-image, the more shadow self you will very likely have. Conversely, the more you live out of your shadow self, the less capable you are of recognizing the persona you are trying to protect and project. It is like a double blindness keeping you from seeing—and being—your best and deepest self. As Jesus put it, "If the lamp within you is, in fact, darkness, what darkness there will be" (Matthew 6:23).

I have prayed for years for one good humiliation a day, and then I must watch my reaction to it. In my position, I have no other way of spotting both my well-denied shadow self and my idealized persona. I am actually surprised there are not more clergy scandals, because "spiritual leader" or "professional religious person" is such a dangerous and ego-inflating self-image. Whenever ministers, or any true believers, are too anti anything, you can be pretty sure there is some shadow material lurking somewhere nearby.

Your persona is what most people want from you and reward you for, and what you choose to identify with, for some reason. As you do your inner work, you will begin to know that your self-*image* is nothing more than just that, and not worth protecting, promoting, or denying. As Jesus says in the passage above, if you can begin to "make friends" with those who have a challenging message for you, you will usually begin to see some of your own shadow. If you don't, you will miss out on much-needed wisdom and end up "imprisoned" within yourself or taken to "court" by others; and you will undoubtedly have to "pay the last penny" to reorder your life and your relationships. Think of our many politicians and clergy who have fallen into public disgrace following sexual and financial scandals.

The "opponent taking you to court" is for me a telling description of what we allow inner story lines to do to us. In ten seconds, we can create an entire and self-justifying scenario of blame, anger, and hurt—toward ourselves or toward another. Jesus is saying, Don't go there! or the judge, officer, and courtroom will quickly take over and have their way with you. Buddhist nun and writer Pema Chodron says that once you create a self-justifying story line, your emotional entrapment within it quadruples! She is surely right, yet I still do it every day, and become my own worst, judge, attorney, and jury within ten seconds of an offending statement.

Your self-image is not substantial or lasting; it is just created out of your own mind, desire, and choice—and everybody else's preferences for you! It floats around in

Plato's unreal world of ideas. It is not objective at all but entirely subjective (which does not mean that it does not have real influence). The movement to second-half-of-life wisdom has much to do with necessary shadow work and the emergence of healthy self-critical thinking, which alone allows you to see beyond your own shadow and disguise and to find who you are "hidden [with Christ] in God," as Paul puts it (Colossians 3:3). The Zen masters call it "the face you had before you were born." This self cannot die and always lives, and is your True Self.

As Jesus put it, "You must recognize the plank in your own eye, and only then will you see clearly enough to take the splinter out of your brother or sister's eye" (Matthew 7:5). He also said, "The lamp of the body is the eye" (Luke 11:34). Spiritual maturity is largely a growth in seeing; and full seeing seems to take most of our lifetime, with a huge leap in the final years, months, weeks, and days of life, as any hospice volunteer will tell you. There seems to be a cumulative and exponential growth in seeing in people's last years, for those who do their inner work. There is also a cumulative closing down in people who have denied all shadow work and humiliating self-knowledge. Watch the Nuremburg trials and see Nazi men who killed millions still in total denial and maintenance of their moral self-image till the very end. I am sure you all know examples of both of these types.

Shadow work is humiliating work, but properly so. If you do not "eat" such humiliations with regularity and make friends with the judges, the courtrooms, and the officers (that is, all those who reveal to you and convict you of your own denied faults) who come into your life, you will surely remain in the first half of life forever. We never get to the second half of life without major shadowboxing. And I am sorry to report that it continues until the end of life, the only difference being that you are no longer surprised by your surprises or so totally humiliated by your humiliations! You come to expect various forms of halfheartedness, deceit, vanity, or illusions from yourself. But now you see through them, which destroys most of their game and power.

Odysseus had to face his same poor judgment again and again; he and others suffered much because of it, yet he usually seemed to learn from his shadow side too. Some call this pattern the discovery of the "golden shadow" because it carries so much enlightenment for the soul. The general pattern in story and novel is that heroes learn and grow from encountering their shadow, whereas villains never do. Invariably, the movies and novels that are most memorable show real "character development" and growing through shadow work. This inspires us all because it calls us all.

We all identify with our persona so strongly when we are young that we become masters of denial and learn to eliminate or deny anything that doesn't support it. *Neither our persona nor our shadow is evil in itself; they just allow us to do evil and not know it.* Our shadow self makes us all into hypocrites on some level. Remember, *hypocrite* is a Greek word that simply means "actor," someone playing a role rather than being "real." We are all in one kind of closet or another and are even encouraged by society to play our roles. Usually everybody else can see your shadow, so it is crucial that you learn what everybody else knows about you—except you!

The saint is precisely one who has no "I" to protect or project. His or her "I" is in conscious union with the "I AM" of God, and that is more than enough. Divine union overrides any need for self-hatred or self-rejection. Such people do not need to be perfectly right, and they know they cannot be anyway; so they just try to be in *right relationship*. In other words, they try above all else to be loving. Love holds you tightly and safely and always. Such people have met the enemy and know that the major enemy is "me," as Pogo said. But you do not hate "me" either, you just see through and beyond "me." Shadow work literally "saves you from yourself" (your false self), which is the foundational meaning of salvation to begin with.

I am afraid that the closer you get to the Light, the more of your shadow you see. Thus truly holy people are *always* humble people. Christians could have been done a great service if shadow had been distinguished from sin. Sin and shadow are not the same. We were so encouraged to avoid sin that many of us instead avoided facing our shadow, and then we ended up "sinning" even worse—while unaware besides! As Paul taught, "The angels of darkness must disguise themselves as angels of light" (2 Corinthians 11:14). The persona does not choose to see evil in itself, so it always disguises it as good. The shadow self invariably presents itself as something like prudence, common sense, justice, or "I am doing this for your good," when it is actually manifesting fear, control, manipulation, or even vengeance. Did anyone ever tell you that the name Lucifer literally means the "light bearer"? The evil one always makes darkness look like light—and makes light look like darkness.

Invariably when something upsets you, and you have a strong emotional reaction out of proportion to the moment, your shadow self has just been exposed. So watch for any overreactions or overdenials. When you notice them, notice also that the cock of St. Peter has just crowed! The reason that a mature or saintly person can be so peaceful, so accepting of self and others, is that there is not much hidden shadow self left. (There is always and forever a little more, however! No exceptions. Shadow work never stops.) This denied and disguised self takes so much energy to face, awaken, and transform all one's life that you have little time to project your fear, anger, or unlived life onto terrorists, Muslims, socialists, liberals, conservatives, or even hate radio.

As the shadows of things continue to show themselves (shadow, even in the physical universe, is created by an admixture of darkness and light), you lose interest in idealizing or idolizing persons or events, especially yourself. You no longer "give away your inner gold" to others. You keep yours, and you let them keep theirs. That does not mean you stop loving other people; in fact, it means you actually start. It does not mean self-hatred or self-doubt, but exactly the contrary, because you finally accept both your gold and your weaknesses as your own—and they no longer cancel one another out. You can finally do the same for others too, and you do not let one or another fault in a person destroy your larger relationship. Here you understand the absolute importance of contemplative or nondualistic thinking, which we will talk about in a bit.

The gift of shadowboxing is in the *seeing* of the shadow and its games, which takes away much of the shadow's hidden power. No wonder that Teresa of Avila said that the mansion of true self-knowledge was the necessary first mansion. Once you have faced your own hidden or denied self, there is not much to be anxious about anymore, because there is no fear of exposure—to yourself or others. The game is over—and you are free. You have now become the "holy fool" of legend and story, which Paul seems to say is the final stage (2 Corinthians 11), when there is no longer any persona to protect or project. You finally are who you are, and can be who you are, without disguise or fear.

DEPRESSION AND SADNESS

There will always be some degree of sadness, humiliation, and disappointment resulting from shadow work, so it's best to learn to recognize it and not obsess over it. It is the false self that is sad and humbled, because its game is over. Holy sadness, once called compunction, is the price your soul pays for opening to the new and the unknown in yourself and in the world. A certain degree of such necessary sadness (another form of necessary suffering!) is important to feel, to accept, and to face.

In our work with men, we have found that in many men this inability or refusal to feel their deep sadness takes the form of aimless anger.[1] The only way to get to the bottom of their anger is to face the ocean of sadness underneath it. Men are not free to cry, so they just transmute their tears into anger, and sometimes it pools up in their soul in the form of real depression. Men are actually encouraged to deny their shadow self in any competitive society, so we all end up with a lot of sad and angry old men. Men are capable of so much more, if they will only do some shadowboxing.

But let me distinguish good and necessary sadness from some forms of depression. *Many depressed people are people who have never taken any risks, never moved outside their comfort zone, never faced necessary suffering, and so their unconscious knows that they have never lived—or loved!* It is not the same as necessary sadness, although it can serve that function. I am afraid that a large percentage of people in their later years are merely depressed or angry. What an unfortunate way to live one's final years.

One of the great surprises is that humans come to full consciousness precisely by shadowboxing, facing their own contradictions, and making friends with their own mistakes and failings. People who have had no inner struggles are invariably both superficial and uninteresting. We tend to endure them more than communicate with them, because they have little to communicate. Shadow work is almost another name for falling upward. Lady Julian put it best of all: "First there is the fall, and then we recover from the fall. Both are the mercy of God!"

CHAPTER 12

NEW PROBLEMS
AND NEW DIRECTIONS

 Learn and obey the rules very well, so you will know how to break them properly.
—THE DALAI LAMA

I f you are on course at all, your world should grow much larger in the second half of life. But I must tell you that, in yet another paradox, your circle of real confidants and truly close friends will normally grow smaller, but also more intimate. You are no longer surprised or angered when most people — and even most institutions — are doing first-half-of-life tasks. In fact, that is what most groups and institutions, and young people, are programmed to do! Don't hate them for it.

Institutions must by necessity be concerned with membership requirements, policies, procedures, protocols, and precedents. If they are working organizations, they need to have very clear criteria for hiring and firing, for supervision and management, and have rules for promotion and salaries. They have to be seriously concerned about lawsuits and litigation. You would resent them even more if they did not do these things well, but *these are nevertheless ego needs and not soul needs.* That is our common dilemma, and it is not easily resolved. But it can be a very creative tension.

We avoid this necessary and creative tension when we try to resolve and end it with old shibboleths like "In the real world . . ." or "On the bottom line . . ." Much of the Gospel has been avoided by such easy dismissals of soul wisdom, which is seldom first of all practical, efficient, or revenue generating. *The bottom line of the Gospel is that most of us have to hit some kind of bottom before we even start the real spiritual journey.* Up to that point, it is mostly religion. At the bottom, there is little time or interest in being totally practical, efficient, or revenue generating. You just want to breathe fresh air. The true Gospel is always fresh air and spacious breathing room.

So our question now becomes, "How can I honor the legitimate needs of the first half of life, while creating space, vision, time, and grace for the second?" *The holding of this tension is the very shape of wisdom.* Only hermits and some retired people can almost totally forget the first and devote themselves totally to the second, but even they must eat, drink, and find housing and clothing! The human art form is in uniting fruitful activity with a contemplative stance — not one or the other, but always both at the same time.[1]

Groups of any kind have to be concerned with such practical things, but that is exactly why you will become impatient with such institutions, including the church, as you grow older and wiser. The implications are staggering. Historically, in the Catholic and Orthodox traditions, you just went off to the side and became a monk or a nun, but now even religious life suffers from the same institutionalization, and is not always a satellite of freedom or the wisdom school that it was meant to be. We have been "churchified," I am afraid.

It is very rare to really absorb the Gospel or wisdom thinking in the first half of life, so we settle for "answers" and organizations, and build the whole structure around such *non-answer answers*. You cannot turn the other cheek if you are an American, nor can you have Eucharistic table fellowship with non-Catholics if you are a Catholic. You end up denying the first and deeper river for the sake of the small river that everybody happens to be floating on. In fact, you just try to improve the barges, boats, and bridges on this small upper river so that people can float more comfortably. The Catholic Church is now expending huge amounts of effort and time changing words in the liturgy back to the "original Latin" (which Jesus never spoke and was actually the language of his oppressors), while the world is facing unparalleled disasters at every level. The sanctuary is the only world where the clergy still have a bit of control, it seems. So again the meticulous navigating of our small river surpasses ever diving into the Big River.

It makes me wonder if Jesus' first definition of church as "two or three gathered in my name" is not still the

best way to avoid these sorts of illusions (Matthew 18:20).
So many people I know who are doing truly helpful and
healing ministry find their primary support from a couple
of enlightened friends—and only secondarily, if at all,
from the larger organization. Larger institutions might well
provide the skeleton, but the muscle, meat, and miracles
invariably happen at the local level.

The ego—and most institutions—demand a tit-for-
tat universe, while the soul swims in a sea of abundance,
grace, and freedom, which cannot always be organized.
Remember, in the Gospel, at the end of the day, the employer
pays those who worked part of a day just as much as those
who worked the whole day (Matthew 20:1–16). This does
not compute except at the level of soul. Soulful people
temper our tantrums by their calm, lessen our urgency
by their peace, exhibit a world of options and alternatives
when all the conversation turns into dualistic bickering.

Soulful people are the necessary salt, yeast, and light
needed to grow groups up (Matthew 5:13–16). Note that
Jesus does not demand that we be the whole meal, the full
loaf, or the illuminated city itself, but we are to be the quiet
undertow and overglow that makes all of these happen.
This is why all institutions need second-half-of-life people
in their ranks; just "two or three" in each organization are
enough to keep them from total self-interest.

If there are not a few soulful people in each group, you
can be sure that those who come at the end of the day, who

are at the back of the line, or who live on the edge of what we call normal will never get paid. Sadly, that seems to be the direction of both our politics and our churches. So we have to prepare and equip the two or three second-half-of-lifers in how to stay in there with mostly first-half-of-lifers! That is surely what Jesus meant by "carrying the cross."

When I say that almost all groups and institutions are first-half-of-life structures, I say that not to discourage you but in fact just the opposite. I say it first of all because it is true, but also to keep you from being depressed or losing all hope by having false expectations. Don't expect or demand from groups what they usually cannot give. Doing so will make you needlessly angry and reactionary. *They must and will be concerned* with identity, boundaries, self-maintenance, self-perpetuation, and self-congratulation. This is their nature and purpose. The most you can hope for is a few enlightened leaders and policies now and then from among those "two or three gathered in my name."

In your second half of life, you can actually bless others in what they feel they must do, allow them to do what they must do, challenge them if they are hurting themselves or others—but you can no longer join them in the first half of life. You can belong to such institutions for all the good that they do, but you no longer put all your eggs in that one basket. This will keep you and others from unnecessary frustration and anger, and from knocking on doors that cannot be opened from the other side. In short, this is what I mean by "emerging Christianity."[2]

Even Jesus said that it would be a waste of time to throw our seeds on the busy footpath, the rocky soil, or among the thorns. He told us we should wait for receptive soil (Matthew 13:4–9). I call such people multipliers, contemplatives, or change agents. Today, I often find this receptive soil more outside of churches than within, many of which have lost that necessary "beginner's mind" both as groups and as individuals. Yet Jesus predicted it himself: "The children of this world are often more clever than the children of light" (Luke 16:8), which is probably why he made the sinner, the outsider, the Gentile, the Samaritan, the woman, the Roman centurion, the poor person, and the leper the heroes and heroines of his stories.

With so many good and sincere people in their ranks, the only way you can explain why the religions formed in the name of Moses, Jesus, and Mohammed became groups that defined themselves by exclusion and "againstness" is that history up to now has largely been asking first-half-of-life questions. It is always interesting to me that the "power of the keys" that Jesus gave to Peter both to "bind and to loose" (Matthew 16:19) is invariably used to bind and so seldom used to loose—unless it is to the church institution's advantage. But when I remember that the first half of life defines itself by "no" and the second half of life by "yes," I can understand. I am grateful that Jesus himself was a teacher from the second half of life, who, according to Paul, "always said yes" (2 Corinthians 2:20).

LONELINESS AND SOLITUDE

There is a certain real loneliness if you say yes and all your old friends are saying no. So be prepared when your old groups, friendships, and even churches no longer fully speak to you the way they used to. But I promise you that those confusing feelings are far outdistanced by a new ability to be alone—and to be happy alone. One of the great surprises at this point is that you find that *the cure for your loneliness is actually solitude!* Who would have imagined that to be the case? I am writing this now in my Lenten hermitage, alone for most of forty days. I could not be happier, more united with everybody else, prayerfully united with the tragic sense of life on this planet, and yet totally "productive" too. Most cannot imagine this, I guess, but it is a different level and a different quality of productivity. Once a person moves to deep time, he or she is utterly one with the whole communion of saints and sinners, past and future. (By the way, I think that is a good way to understand reincarnation!) In deep time, everybody matters and has his or her influence, and is even somehow "present" and not just past.

Basically, the first half of life is writing the text, and the second half is writing the commentary on that text. We all tend to move toward a happy and needed introversion as we get older. Such introversion is necessary to unpack all that life has given us and taken from us. We engage in what is now a necessary and somewhat natural contemplation. We should not be surprised that most older people do not choose loud music, needless diversions, or large crowds. We move toward understimulation, if we are on the schedule of soul. Life has stimulated us enough, and now we have to process it and integrate it, however unconsciously. Silence and poetry start being our more natural voice and our more beautiful ear at this stage.[3] Much of life starts becoming highly symbolic and "connecting," and little things become significant metaphors for everything else. Silence is the only language spacious enough to include everything and to keep us from slipping back into dualistic judgments and divisive words.

Poets like Gerard Manley Hopkins, Mary Oliver, David Whyte, Denise Levertov, Naomi Shihab Nye, Rainer Maria Rilke, and T. S. Eliot now name your own inner experience, even if you have never read poetry before. Mystics like Rumi, Hafiz, Kabir, John of the Cross, Therese of Lisieux, Baal Shem Tov, Lady Julian of Norwich, and Rabia will speak to you perhaps more than people from your own tradition — whereas before you did not know, or did not care, what they were talking about. Like Jesus, you may soon feel as though you have "nowhere to lay your head," while a whole set of new heads are now making sense to you! This is true politically too. In fact, if your politics do not become more compassionate and inclusive, I doubt whether you are on the second journey.

This is initially quite scary, but the issue is no longer "Is she or he in my group, my country, my political party, my social class?" but "Has she or he 'passed over' to the Big Picture?" Members of this new "nongroup group" can talk to one another rather easily, it seems. What some now call "emerging Christianity" or "the emerging church" is not something you join, establish, or invent. You just name it and then you see it everywhere—already in place! Such nongroup groups, the "two or three" gathered in deeper truth, create a whole new level of affiliation, dialogue, and friendship, even though they can still enjoy being among their old friends too, as long as they do not talk about anything serious, political, or religious.

A kind of *double belonging* is characteristic of people at this stage. No one group meets all of their needs, desires, and visions. I bet that if you've lasted this long with this book, you yourself are a "double belonger," maybe even a triple or more! Colonized people, oppressed people, every kind of minority have had to learn several levels of belonging to survive and get through the day; for us more comfortable folks it is still a stretch, but finally a stretch that many are making, perhaps without even realizing it.

BOTH-AND THINKING

What this illustrates, of course, is a newly discovered capacity for what many religions have called "nondualistic thinking" or both-and thinking.[4] It is almost the benchmark of our growth into the second half of life. More calm and contemplative seeing does not appear suddenly, but grows almost unconsciously over many years of conflict, confusion, healing, broadening, loving, and forgiving reality. It emerges gradually as we learn to "incorporate the negative," learn from what we used to exclude, or, as Jesus put it, "forgive the enemies" both within and without.

You no longer need to divide the field of every moment between up and down, totally right or totally wrong, with me or against me. It just *is. This calm allows you to confront what must be confronted with even greater clarity and incisiveness.* This stance is not passivity at all. It is, in fact, the essential link between true contemplation and skillful action. The big difference is that your small and petty self is out of the way, and if God wants to use you, which God always does, God's chances are far better now!

Dualistic thinking is the well-practiced pattern of knowing most things by comparison. And for some reason, once you compare or label things (that is, judge), you almost always conclude that one is good and the other is less good or even bad. Don't take my word for it; just notice your own thoughts and reactions. You will see that you will move almost automatically into a pattern of up or down, in or out, for me or against me, right or wrong, black or white, gay or straight, good or bad. It is the basic reason why the "stinking thinking" of racism, sexism, classism, homophobia, religious imperialism, and prejudice of all kinds is so hard to overcome and has lasted so long—even among nice people!

At the risk of being too cleverly alliterative (though it may help you remember), here is the normal sequencing of the dualistic mind: *it compares, it competes, it conflicts, it conspires, it condemns, it cancels out any contrary evidence, and it then crucifies with impunity.* You can call it the seven C's of delusion, and the source of most violence, which is invariably *sacralized* as good and necessary to "make the world safe for democracy" or to "save souls for heaven."

Nondualistic or contemplative thinking was put off or fully denied in the first half of life for the sake of quickly drawn ego boundaries and clear goals, which created a nice clean "provisional personality." Dualistic thinking works only for a while to get us started, but if we are honest, it stops being helpful in most real-life situations. It is fine for teenagers to really think that there is some moral or "supernatural" superiority to their chosen baseball team, their army, their ethnic group, or even their religion; but one hopes they learn that such polarity thinking is recognized as just an agreed-upon game by the second half of life. Your frame should grow larger as you move toward the

Big Picture in which one God creates all and loves all, both Dodgers and Yankees, blacks and whites, Palestinians and Jews, Americans and Afghanis.

The trouble is that a lot of people don't get there! We are often so attached to our frame, game, and raft that it becomes a substitute for objective truth, because it is all we have! Inside such entrapment, most people do not see things as they *are;* rather, they see things as *they* are. In my experience, this is most of the world, unless people have done their inner work, at least some shadow work, and thereby entered into wisdom, or nondualistic thinking. Through centuries of meticulous and utterly honest self-observation, Buddhism has helped people see this in themselves probably better than most of the world religions. Jesus saw it, but we did not see him very well.

In the first half of life, the negative, the mysterious, the scary, and the problematic are always exported elsewhere. Doing so gives you a quick and firm ego structure that works for a while. But such splitting *is not an objective statement of truth!* It is just helpful for your private purposes. Eventually this overcompensation in one direction must be resolved and balanced. This integration, or "forgiveness of everything" as I like to call it, is the very name of growth, maturity, and holiness.

In the second half of life, all that you avoided for the sake of a manufactured ego ideal starts coming back as a true friend and teacher. Doers become thinkers, feelers become doers, thinkers become feelers, extroverts become introverts, visionaries become practical, and the practical ones long for vision. We all go toward the very places we avoided for the last forty years, and our friends are amazed. Now we begin to understand why Jesus is always welcoming the outsider, the foreigner, the sinner, the wounded one. He was a second-half-of-life man who has had the unenviable task of trying to teach and be understood by a largely first-half-of-life history, church, and culture.

Listen to his dangerous and inclusionary thinking: "My Father's sun shines on the good and the bad, his rain falls on the just and the unjust" (Matthew 5:45). Or "Don't pull out the weeds or you might pull out the wheat along with it. Let the weeds and the wheat both grow together until the harvest" (Matthew 13:29–30). If I had presented such fuzzy thinking in my moral theology class, I would have gotten an F!

Jesus, I am convinced, was the first nondualistic religious thinker in the West (there were philosophers like Heraclitus), but his teachings were quickly filtered through Greek dualistic logic! Nondualistic wisdom is just not helpful when you are trying to form a strong group, clarify first principles, or demonstrate that your idea is superior to others' ideas. At that stage, real wisdom appears to be pious and dangerous poetry. And at that necessary early stage, such warnings are probably right! But that is also why clergy and spiritual teachers need to be second-half-of-life people, and why so many of us have mangled, manipulated, and minimized the brilliance of Jesus when we heard him in our early stage of development.

So we need first to clarify before we can subtly discriminate. Dualistic thinking gets you in the right ball park ("You cannot serve both God and mammon"), but nondualistic wisdom, or what many of us call *contemplation*, is necessary once you actually get in the right field. "Now that I have chosen to serve God, what does that really mean?" Nondualistic thinking presumes that you have first mastered dualistic clarity, but also found it *insufficient* for the really big issues like love, suffering, death, God, and any notion of infinity. In short, we need *both*.

Unless you let the truth of life teach you on its own terms, unless you develop some concrete practice for recognizing and overcoming your dualistic mind, you will remain in the first half of life forever, as most of humanity has up to now. In the first half of life, you cannot work with the imperfect, nor can you accept the tragic sense of life, which finally means that you cannot love anything or anyone at any depth. Nothing is going to change in history as long as most people are merely dualistic, either-or thinkers. Such splitting and denying leaves us at the level of mere information, data, facts, and endlessly arguing about the same. "My facts are better than your facts," we yell at ever higher volume and with ever stronger ego attachment.

Wisdom was distinguished from mere knowledge by Isaiah (11:2), by Paul (1 Corinthians 12:8–9), and by Scholastic philosophy, which spoke of analytic intelligence and intuitive or "connatural" intelligence ("like knows like") as two very different levels of consciousness. We live in a time when we are finally free to appreciate how right they all were.

Now much of modern science recognizes the very real coherence between the seer and what is seen or even can be seen. *Wisdom seeing has always sought to change the seer first, and then knows that what is seen will largely take care of itself*. It is almost that simple, and it is always that hard.

Whole people see and create wholeness wherever they go; split people see and create splits in everything and everybody. By the second half of our lives, we are meant to see in wholes and no longer just in parts. Yet we get to the whole by falling *down* into the messy parts — so many times, in fact, that we long and thirst for the wholeness and fullness of all things, including ourselves. I promise you this unified field is the only and lasting meaning of *up*.

CHAPTER 13

FALLING UPWARD

How surely gravity's law,
strong as an ocean current,
takes hold of even the smallest thing
and pulls it toward the heart of the world. . . .
This is what the things can teach us:
to fall,
patiently to trust our heaviness.
—RAINER MARIA RILKE, *BOOK OF HOURS*

Most of us tend to think of the second half of life as largely about getting old, dealing with health issues, and letting go of our physical life, but the whole thesis of this book is exactly the opposite. What looks like falling can largely be experienced as falling upward and onward, into a broader and deeper world, where the soul has found its fullness, is finally connected to the whole, and lives inside the Big Picture.

It is not a loss but somehow a gain, not losing but actually winning. You probably have to have met at least one true elder to imagine that this could be true. I have met enough radiant people in my life to know that it is fairly common. They have come to their human fullness, often against all odds, and usually by suffering personally or vicariously. As Jesus describes such a person, "from their breasts flow fountains of living water" (John 7:38). These are the models and goals for our humanity, much more than the celebrities and politicos whom we care so much about today.

I recently watched a documentary on the life of the blind and deaf woman, Helen Keller. She seems to have leaped into the second half of life in the chronological first half of her life, once she discovered her depths and despite her severe limitations. She lived an entire life of rather amazing happiness and generativity for others. She was convinced that life was about service to others and not about protecting or lamenting her supposedly handicapped body.

That seems to be the great difference between transformed and nontransformed people. Great people come to serve, not to be served. It is the twelfth and final and necessary step of the inspired Twelve Steps of Alcoholics Anonymous. *Until and unless you give your life away to others, you do not seem to have it yourself at any deep level.* Good parents always learn that. Many of the happiest, most generous and focused people I know are young mothers. This is another one of those utter paradoxes! We seem to be "mirrored" into life by the response, love, and needed challenge of others. Thank God Anne Sullivan knew how to beautifully mirror Helen Keller, at great loving cost to herself. We all need at least one such mirror if we are to thrive.

MIRRORING

Somewhere in my late forties, I realized that many people loved and admired me for who I was not, and many people also resented or rejected me for who I was not. Conversely, many loved me for who I really was, warts and all, and *this was the only love that ever redeemed me.* Many others rightly criticized me for who I really was, and revealed to me my shadow, which was always painful but often very helpful. But in all cases, it became apparent that their responses said much more about *them* and the good or bad quality of their own mirroring than about me at all!

Beauty or ugliness really *is* first of all in the eye of the beholder. Good people will mirror goodness in us, which is why we love them so much. Not-so-mature people will mirror their own unlived and confused life onto us, which is why they confuse and confound us so much, and why they are hard to love.

At any rate, it is only those who respond to *the real you, good or bad,* that help you in the long run. Much of the work of midlife is learning to tell the difference between people who are still dealing with *their issues through you* and those who are really dealing with *you as you really are.* As an older man, carrying the priest title of "Father" besides, I find that I am often carrying people's "daddy" projections, both for good and for ill. It is a double-edged sword, because I can be used to heal them very easily, and

I can be allowed to hurt them very easily. But in a certain real sense, it is not about *me* at all but about me as their mirror, reflection, and projection.

By the second half of life, you learn to tell the difference between who you really are and how others can mirror that or not. This will keep you from taking either insults or praise too seriously. I doubt whether this kind of calm discrimination and detachment is much possible before your midfifties at the earliest. How desperately we need true elders in our world to clean up our seeing and stop the revolving hall of mirrors in its tracks.

We all take what we need, get what we want, and reject what we shouldn't from one another. Don't accept your first responses at face value. The only final and meaningful question is "Is it true?" Not "Who said it?" "When and where did they say it?" "Does the Bible or the pope or my president say it?" or "Do I like it?" The only meaningful, helpful, and humble question is "Is it objectively true?"

In the second half of life, you gradually step out of this hall of revolving and self-reflecting mirrors. You can usually do this well only if you have *one true mirror yourself,* at least one loving, honest friend to ground you, which might even be the utterly accepting gaze of the Friend. But, by all means, you must find at least one true mirror that reveals your inner, deepest, and, yes, divine image. This is why intimate moments are often mirroring moments of beautiful mutual receptivity, and why such intimacy heals us so deeply.

Thinking you can truthfully mirror yourself is a first-half-of-life illusion. Mature spirituality has invariably insisted on soul friends, gurus, confessors, mentors, masters, and spiritual directors for individuals, and prophets and truth speakers for groups and institutions.

My Franciscan sister St. Clare of Assisi (1194–1253) seems to have found the mirror to be her most frequent and helpful image for what she saw happening in the spiritual life. She loved to advise her sisters to variously "Place yourself before the mirror," "Let the Light mirror you," and "Look upon the mirror [of perfect love] each day." She clearly understood that *spiritual gifts are always reflected gifts*. Clare predated Heinz Kohut's "self psychology" and our present knowledge of mirror neurons by eight centuries. *Mystics often intuit and live what scientists later prove to be true.*

We really do find ourselves through one another's eyes, and only when that has been done truthfully can we mirror others with freedom, truth, and compassion. Jesus himself predated Clare by twelve centuries when he said, "The lamp of the body is the eye. If your eye is healthy, your whole body will be filled with light" (Matthew 6:22). It is all a matter of learning how to see, and it takes much of our life to learn to see well and truthfully.

In the second half of life, people have less power to infatuate you, but they also have much less power to control you or hurt you. It is the freedom of the second half *not* to need. Both the ecstatic mirroring of my youth and the mature and honest mirroring of my adulthood have held up what I needed to see and could see at the time; they have prepared me for the fully compassionate and Divine Mirror, who has always shown me to myself in times and ways that I could handle and enjoy. I fell many times relationally, professionally, emotionally, and physically in my life, but there was always a trampoline effect that allowed me to finally fall upward. No falling down was final, but actually contributed to the bounce!

God knows that all of us will fall somehow. Those events that lead us to "catastrophize" out of all proportion must be business as usual for God — at least six billion times a day. Like good spiritual directors do, God must say after each failure of ours, "Oh, here is a great opportunity! Let's see how we can work with this!" After our ego-inflating successes, God surely says, "Well, nothing new or good is going to happen here!" Failure and suffering are the great equalizers and levelers among humans. Success is just the opposite. Communities and commitment can form around suffering much more than around how wonderful or superior we are. Just compare the real commitment to one another, to the world, and to truth in "happy clappy religion" with the deep solidarity of families at the time of a tragic death or among hospice workers and their clients. There is a strange and even wonderful communion in real human pain, actually much more than in joy, which is too often manufactured and passing. In one sense, pain's effects are not passing, and pain is less commonly manufactured. Thus it is a more honest doorway into lasting communion than even happiness.

The genius of the Gospel was that it included the problem inside the solution. The falling became the standing. The stumbling became the finding. The dying became the rising. The raft became the shore. The small self cannot see this very easily, because it doubts itself too much, is still too fragile, and is caught up in the tragedy of it all. It has not lived long enough to see the big patterns. No wonder so many of our young commit suicide. This is exactly why we need elders and those who can mirror life truthfully and foundationally for the young. Intimate I-Thou relationships are the greatest mirrors of all, so we dare not avoid them, but for the young they have perhaps not yet taken place at any depth, so young people are always very fragile.

Many of us discover in times of such falling the Great Divine Gaze, the ultimate I-Thou relationship, which is always compassionate and embracing, or it would not be divine. Like any true mirror, the gaze of God receives us exactly as we are, without judgment or distortion, subtraction or addition. Such *perfect receiving* is what transforms us. Being totally received as we truly are is what we wait and long for all our lives. All we can do is receive and return the loving gaze of God every day, and afterwards we will be internally free and deeply happy at the same time. The One who knows all has no trouble including, accepting, and forgiving all. Soon we who are gazed upon so perfectly can pass on the same accepting gaze to all others who need it. There is no longer any question "Does he or she deserve it?" What we received was totally undeserved itself.

Just remember this: no one can keep you from the second half of your own life except yourself. Nothing can inhibit your second journey except your own lack of courage, patience, and imagination. Your second journey is all yours to walk or to avoid. My conviction is that some falling apart of the first journey is necessary for this to happen, so do not waste a moment of time lamenting poor parenting, lost job, failed relationship, physical handicap, gender identity, economic poverty, or even the tragedy of any kind of abuse. *Pain is part of the deal.* If you don't walk into the second half of your own life, it is *you* who do not want it. God will always give you exactly what you truly want and desire. So make sure you desire, desire deeply, desire yourself, desire God, desire everything good, true, and beautiful.

All the emptying out is only for the sake of a Great Outpouring.

God, like nature, abhors all vacuums, and rushes to fill them.

A MEDITATION ON A POEM
BY THOMAS MERTON

Thomas Merton, the Cistercian monk, who died tragically in 1968, has been a primary teacher and inspiration to me since I first read his book *Sign of Jonah* in a high school seminary library soon after it was written in 1958. I did my first full hermitage at Gethsemani, his Kentucky monastery, during the Easter season in 1985, at the kind invitation of the abbot. I saw Merton once for just a moment, as he walked in front of me while I was visiting the monastery with my parents in early June of 1961, the day I had graduated from high school in Cincinnati. Little did I think he would soon die, or did I imagine the ongoing influence he would have on so many people around the world and on me.

I believe Thomas Merton is probably the most significant American Catholic of the twentieth century, along with Dorothy Day. His whole life is a parable and a paradox, like all of ours are; but he had an uncanny ability to describe his inner life with God for the rest of us. His best-selling *Seven Storey Mountain* is a first-half-of-life statement, which has never gone out of print since 1948. It is brilliant in its passion, poetry, discovery, and newly found ecstasy, yet it is still rather dualistic. The following poem, "When in the Soul of the Serene Disciple," written ten years later, shows all the signs of a man in an early second half of life, although he was only in his midforties. I offer it as an appropriate closing for our journey together. The freedom illustrated here might be exactly where the further journey is going to lead you. I hope so.

When in the Soul of the Serene Disciple

When in the soul of the serene disciple
With no more Fathers to imitate
Poverty is a success,
It is a small thing to say the roof is gone:
He has not even a house.

Stars, as well as friends,
Are angry with the noble ruin.
Saints depart in several directions.

Be still:
There is no longer any need of comment.
It was a lucky wind

That blew away his halo with his cares,
A lucky sea that drowned his reputation.

Here you will find
Neither a proverb nor a memorandum.
There are no ways,
No methods to admire
Where poverty is no achievement.
His God lives in his emptiness like an affliction.

What choice remains?
Well, to be ordinary is not a choice:
It is the usual freedom
Of men without visions.[1]

This poem has spoken to me from the first time I read it in his hermitage in 1985, and I offer it to you as a simple meditation that you can return to again and again to summarize where this journey has led us.

When in the soul of the serene disciple

At the soul level, and with the peacefulness of time

With no more Fathers to imitate

When you have moved beyond the "authoritative," the collective, and the imitative, and you have to be your True Self

Poverty is a success,
It is a small thing to say the roof is gone:
He has not even a house.

> *When you have made it all the way to the bottom of*
> *who you think you are, or need to be, when your*
> *humiliating shadow work never stops, and when your*
> *securities and protective boundaries mean less and less,*
> *and your "salvation project" has failed you*

Stars, as well as friends,
Are angry with the noble ruin,
Saints depart in several directions.

> *When you have faced the hurt and the immense*
> *self-doubt brought on by good people, family, and even*
> *friends who do not understand you, who criticize you,*
> *or even delight at your wrongness*

Be still:
There is no longer any need of comment.

> *The inner life of quiet, solitude, and contemplation is*
> *the only way to find your ground and purpose now. Go*
> *nowhere else for sustenance.*

It was a lucky wind
That blew away his halo with his cares,

A lucky sea that drowned his reputation.

> *This is the necessary stumbling stone that makes you*
> *loosen your grip on the first half of life and takes away*
> *any remaining superior self-image. (Merton is calling*
> *this crossover point "lucky" and surely sees it as part of*
> *necessary and good suffering that the soul needs in*
> *order to mature.)*

Here you will find
Neither a proverb nor a memorandum.
There are no ways,
No methods to admire

> *Don't look forward or backward in your mind for*
> *explanations or consolations; don't try to hide behind*
> *any secret special way that you have practiced and now*
> *can recommend to all! (As we preachy types always feel*
> *we must do.) Few certitudes now, just naked faith.*

Where poverty is no achievement.
His God lives in his emptiness like an affliction.

> *This is nothing you have come to or crawled down to by*
> *effort or insight. You were taken there, and your*
> *"there" is precisely nothing. (That is, it is "everything,"*
> *but not what you expected everything to be!) This kind*
> *of God is almost a disappointment, at least to those who*

were in any way "using" God up to now. There is
nothing to claim anymore. God is not a possession of
any type, not for your own ego or morality or
superiority or for control of the data. This is the "nada"
of John of the Cross and the mystics, and this is Jesus on
the cross. Yet it is a peaceful nothingness and a
luminous darkness, while still an "affliction."

What choice remains?
Well, to be ordinary is not a choice:
It is the usual freedom
Of men [and women] without [their] visions.

In the second half of the spiritual life, you are not
making choices as much as you are being guided,
taught, and led — which leads to "choiceless choices."
These are the things you cannot not *do because of what*
you have become, things you do not need to do because
they are just not yours to do, and things you absolutely
must *do because they are your destiny and your deepest*
desire. Your driving motives are no longer money,
success, or the approval of others. You have found your
sacred dance.

Now your only specialness is in being absolutely
ordinary and even "choiceless," beyond the strong
opinions, needs, preferences, and demands of the first
half of life. You do not need your "visions" anymore;
you are happily participating in God's vision for you.

*With that, the wonderful dreaming and the dreamer
that we were in our early years have morphed into
Someone Else's dream for us. We move from the
driver's seat to being a happy passenger, one who is still
allowed to make helpful suggestions to the Driver. We
are henceforth "a serene disciple," living in our own
unique soul as never before, yet paradoxically living
within the mind and heart of God, and taking our place
in the great and general dance.*

Amen, Alleluia!

Bible versions: I studied from the *Jerusalem Bible,* I have made use of the *New American Bible,* and I often read *The Message* to get a new slant on a passage, but the edited form I use is often my own translation or a combination of the above.

The Invitation to a Further Journey

1. I am going to take the liberty of capitalizing this term throughout this book so you will know that I am not referring to the small self or psychological self, but the larger and foundational self that we are in God.

2. John Duns Scotus (1266–1308) was the Franciscan philosopher who most influenced Thomas Merton and Gerard Manley Hopkins, and all of us who love his subtle arguments for divine freedom, a Cosmic Christ, a nonviolent theology of redemption, and, in this poem, his wonderful doctrine of "thisness." For Scotus, God does not create categories, classes, genuses, or species, but only unique and chosen individuals. Everything is a unique "this"! See Ingham, Mary Beth, *Scotus for Dunces* (St. Bonaventure, N.Y.: St. Bonaventure University, 2003); Hopkins, Gerard Manley, *Poems and Prose* (New York: Penguin, 1984), 51.

Introduction

1. Rohr, Richard, *Adam's Return: The Five Promises of Male Initiation* (New York: Crossroad, 2004).

2. Armstrong, Karen, *A Short History of Myth* (Edinburgh: Canongate Books, 2006).

3. Rohr, Richard, *The Naked Now: Learning to See as the Mystics See* (New York: Crossroad, 2009).

4. *The Odyssey,* trans. Samuel Butler (Lawrence, Kans.: Digireads .com Publishing, 2009).

Chapter 1: The Two Halves of Life

1. Maslow, Abraham H., "A Theory of Human Motivation," *Psychological Review,* 1943, developed and revised in many of his later books.

2. Wilber, Ken, *One Taste* (Boston: Shambhala, 2000), 25–28. Although Wilber develops his distinction between the "translative" and the truly "transformative" functions of religion in several places, this is one of the most succinct summaries. Religion must "devastate" before it consoles.

Chapter 2: The Hero and Heroine's Journey

1. Campbell, Joseph, *The Hero with a Thousand Faces* (Princeton, N.J.: Princeton University Press, 1973).

2. Rohr, Richard, *Adam's Return: The Five Promises of Male Initiation* (New York: Crossroad, 2004).

Chapter 3: The First Half of Life

1. Fromm, Eric, *The Art of Loving* (New York: Harper & Row, 1956), 43f.

2. Mander, Jerry, *In the Absence of the Sacred* (San Francisco: Sierra Club Books, 1991).

3. Spiral Dynamics is a theory of human consciousness that claims to "explain everything." In fact, it is quite convincing and helpful in terms of understanding at what level individuals, groups, nations, and whole eras hear, process, and act on their experience. Paralleling the foundational work of Piaget, Maslow, Fowler, Kohlberg, and Clare Graves, people like Robert Kegan, Don Beck, and Ken Wilber have made "Integral Theory" a part of much political, social, and religious discourse. "Transpartisan" thinking would often describe the higher levels of consciousness, whereas many progressive people still think "bipartisan" is as high as we can go. I have used the words *nondualistic thinking,* or *contemplation,* to mean approximately the same.

4. Rohr, Richard, *From Wild Man to Wise Man* (Cincinnati, Ohio: St. Anthony Messenger Press, 2005), 73f.

5. Plotkin, Bill, *Nature and the Human Soul* (Novato, Calif.: New World Library, 2008), 49f. In Plotkin's eight-stage wheel of development, he sees the early stages as largely ego driven, as they have to be. Until we make some kind of "soul encounter" with the deeper self, we cannot be soul drawn and live from our deeper identity. It is a brilliant analysis that parallels our own work in initiation (M.A.L.Es) and my thesis in this book.

6. Plotkin, Bill, *Soulcraft* (Novato, Calif.: New World Library, 2003), 91f.

7. Turner, Victor, *The Ritual Process* (Ithaca, N.Y.: Cornell University, 1977), 94f. This book first clarified for me the concept of liminality, and why spiritual change, transformation, and initiation can happen best when we are on some "threshold" of our own lives. "Liminal space" has since become a key concept in my own work in initiation. Many people avoid all movement

into any kind of liminal space, keep on cruise control, and nothing new happens.

8. May, Gerald, *The Dark Night of the Soul* (New York: Harper-Collins, 2004).

Chapter 4: The Tragic Sense of Life

1. de Unamuno, Miguel, *Tragic Sense of Life* (Mineola, N.Y.: Dover, 1954).

2. Rohr, Richard, *The Enneagram: A Christian Perspective* (New York: Crossroad, 1999). After almost forty years of working with this explanation of human motivation and behavior, I am convinced that it was discovered and refined to help the "discernment of spirits" in spiritual directees. It makes very clear that your "sin" and your gift are two sides of the same coin and that you cannot fully face one without also facing the other. This tool has changed many lives.

3. Brueggemann, Walter, *Theology of the Old Testament* (Minneapolis, Minn.: Fortress Press, 1999), 61f. "Israel's religion, and thus the texts, are incessantly pluralistic," according to both Brueggemann and Professor Rainer Albertz.

Chapter 5: Stumbling over the Stumbling Stone

1. Rohr, Richard, *Things Hidden: Scripture as Spirituality* (Cincinnati, Ohio: St. Anthony Messenger Press), 195f. For Franciscans, Jesus did not need to change the mind of God about humanity, but he came to change the mind of humanity about God. Ours was a Cosmic Christ from all eternity who revealed the eternal love of God on the cross, but God did not need any "payment" to love us.

2. Moore, Robert, *Facing the Dragon* (Wilmette, Ill.: Chiron, 2003), 68f.

Chapter 6: Necessary Suffering

1. Hopkins, Gerard Manley, "That Nature Is a Heraclitean Fire and the Comfort of the Resurrection," *Poems and Prose* (New York: Penguin, 1984), 65f.

2. Merton, Thomas, *New Seeds of Contemplation* (New York: New Directions, 1962), passim. Merton's descriptions of the terms *true self* and *false self* have become a foundational piece of modern spirituality, and have clarified for many what the self is that has to "die" according to Jesus, and what the self is that lives forever.

Chapter 7: Home and Homesickness

1. Jung, Carl G., *The Collected Works of C. G. Jung,* vol. 1, *Psychiatric Studies* (Princeton, N.J.: Princeton University Press, 1980), 483.

2. Christiansen, Michael, and Jeffery Wittung, *Partakers of the Divine Nature* (Madison, N.J.: Fairleigh Dickinson University, 2007). The process of the divinization of human persons, or *theosis,* is for me at the very heart of the meaning of the Christian message, but it has been feared and undeveloped in the Western churches.

Chapter 8: Amnesia and the Big Picture

1. Clement, Olivier, *The Roots of Christian Mysticism: Texts from the Patristic Era with Commentary* (London: New City, 2002). This excellent and profound book is worth reading several

times, and reveals how little the Western churches studied the Eastern Church fathers or the early period at all.

2. Wordsworth, William, "Intimations of Immortality from Recollections of Early Childhood," *Immortal Poems of the English Language* (New York: Washington Square), 260f.

3. General audience, Pope John Paul II, June 28, 1999.

4. Gulley, Philip, and James Mulholland, *If Grace Is True* (New York: HarperCollins, 2004).

Chapter 9: A Second Simplicity

1. Pearce, Joseph Chilton, *The Biology of Transcendence* (Rochester, Vt.: Park Street Press, 2002); Newberg, Andrew, *Why God Won't Go Away* (New York: Ballantine Books, 2002).

2. Butcher, Carmen Adevedo, *The Cloud of Unknowing* (Boston: Shambhala, 2009). This new translation of an enduring classic can serve as the missing link for both modern fundamentalism and atheism, which suffer from the same deficit.

3. Eliot, T. S., "The Dry Salvages," *Four Quartets* (New York: Harcourt, Brace & World, 1971), 39.

4. Rohr, Richard, *Everything Belongs: The Gift of Contemplative Prayer* (New York: Crossroad), 1999.

Chapter 10: A Bright Sadness

1. Augustine, *Confessions,* Book 10, 27, largely my translation.

2. Merton, Thomas, *New Seeds of Contemplation* (New York: New Directions, 1961), 297.

Chapter 11: The Shadowlands

1. Men as Learners and Elders, or M.A.L.Es, is our male spirituality program, which offers men's rites of passage and programs for male enrichment worldwide. See http://malespirituality.org.

Chapter 12: New Problems and New Directions

1. The Center for Action and Contemplation was founded in Albuquerque, New Mexico, in 1987 to help people working for social change to develop a rich interior life; we have always said that the most important word in our long title is "and." See http://cacradicalgrace.org.

2. McLaren, Brian, Phyllis Tickle, Shane Claiborne, Alexie Torres Fleming, and Richard Rohr, "Emerging Christianity" (2010) and "Emerging Church" (2009), recorded conferences, available at http://cacradicalgrace.org.

3. Sardello, Robert, *Silence: The Mystery of Wholeness* (Berkeley, Calif.: Goldenstone Press, 2008); Picard, Max, *The World of Silence* (Washington, D.C.: Regnery Gateway, 1988).

4. Rohr, Richard, *The Naked Now: Learning to See as the Mystics See* (New York: Crossroad, 2009).

Coda

1. Merton, Thomas, *Collected Poems* (New York: New Directions, 1977), 279f.

Armstrong, Karen. *The Bible: The Biography.* London: Atlantic Books, 2007.

Becker, Ernest. *The Denial of Death.* New York: Free Press, 1973.

Bly, Robert. *The Sibling Society.* Reading, Mass.: Addison-Wesley, 1996.

Bourgeault, Cynthia. *Centering Prayer and Inner Awakening.* Cambridge, Mass.: Cowely, 2004.

Buhlmann, Walbert. *The Coming of the Third Church.* Maryknoll, N.Y.: Orbis, 1980.

Butcher, Carmen Acevedo. *The Cloud of Unknowing with the Book of Privy Council: A New Translation.* Boston: Shambhala, 2009.

Campbell, Joseph (ed.). *The Portable Jung.* New York: Penguin, 1971.

Chodron, Pema. *Start Where You Are: A Guide to Compassionate Living.* Boston: Shambhala, 2001.

――. *Comfortable with Uncertainty: 108 Teachings.* Boston: Shambhala, 2006.

Eberle, Scott. *The Final Crossing.* Big Pine, Calif.: Lost Borders Press, 2006.

Fowler, James. *Stages of Faith: The Psychology of Human Development and the Quest for Meaning.* San Francisco: Harper San Francisco, 1995.

Frankl, Viktor. *Man's Search for Meaning.* New York: Washington Square Press, 1984.

Freeman, Laurence. *Jesus: The Teacher Within.* New York: Continuum International, 2000.

Girard, Rene. *The Girard Reader*. (J. Williams, ed.). New York: Crossroad, 1996.

Goleman, Daniel. *Emotional Intelligence: Why It Can Matter More Than IQ*. New York: Bantam Books, 1997.

Grant, Robert. *The Way of the Wound: A Spirituality of Trauma and Transformation*. Burlingame, Calif.: private publisher, 1998.

Gulley, Philip, and James Mulholland. *If Grace Is True: Why God Will Save Every Person*. San Francisco: Harper San Francisco, 2003.

Gunn, Robert Jingen. *Journeys into Emptiness: Dogen, Merton, Jung and the Quest for Transformation*. New York: Paulist Press, 2000.

Hagberg, Janet. *Real Power: The Stages of Personal Power in Organizations*. Minneapolis, Minn.: Winston, 1984.

Hanna, Charles Bartruff. *The Face of the Deep: The Religious Ideas of C. G. Jung*. Philadelphia: Westminister Press, 1967.

Hart, Tobin. *From Information to Transformation: Education for the Evolution of Consciousness*. New York: Lang, 2001.

Hillman, James. *The Soul's Code: In Search of Character and Calling*. New York: Warner Books, 1996.

Hollis, James. *The Middle Passage: From Misery to Meaning in Midlife*. Toronto: Inner City Books, 1993.

———. *Finding Meaning in the Second Half of Life: How to Finally, Really Grow Up*. New York: Gotham Books, 2006.

Inchausti, Robert. *Subversive Orthodoxy: Outlaws, Revolutionaries, and Christians in Disguise*. Grand Rapids, Mich.: Brazos Press, 2005.

James, William. *The Varieties of Religious Experience*. New York: Random House, 1999. (Originally published 1902.)

Johnson, Robert. *Transformation: Understanding the Three Levels of Masculine Consciousness.* San Francisco: Harper San Francisco, 1991.

———. *Inner Gold: Understanding Psychological Projection.* Kihei, Hawaii: Koa Books, 2008.

Johnston, William. *"Arise, My Love . . .": Mysticism for a New Era.* Maryknoll, N.Y.: Orbis, 2008.

Julian of Norwich. (E. Colledge and J. Walsh, trans.). *Julian of Norwich: Showings (Classics of Western Spirituality).* New York: Paulist Press, 1977.

Jung, Carl G. *The Collected Works of C. G. Jung.* Princeton, N.J.: Princeton University Press, 1980.

Katie, Byron. *Loving What Is: Four Questions That Can Change Your Life.* New York: Three Rivers Press, 2002.

———. *A Thousand Names for Joy: Living in Harmony with the Way Things Are.* New York: Harmony, 2007.

Kegan, Robert. *In over Our Heads: The Mental Demands of Modern Life.* Cambridge, Mass.: Harvard University Press, 1994.

Kelsey, Morton. *Discernment: A Study in Ecstasy and Evil.* New York: Paulist Press, 1978.

Lane, Belden. *The Solace of Fierce Landscapes: Exploring Desert and Mountain Spirituality.* New York: Oxford University Press, 1998.

Levinson, Daniel. *The Season of a Man's Life.* New York: Knopf, 1978.

Loy, David. *Nonduality: A Study in Comparative Philosophy.* New Haven, Conn.: Yale University Press, 1988.

Marion, Jim. *Putting on the Mind of Christ: The Inner Work of Spirituality.* Charlottesville, Va.: Hampton Roads, 2000.

Matthew, Iain. *The Impact of God: Soundings from St. John of the Cross.* London: Hodder and Stoughton, 1995.

McColman, Carl. *The Big Book of Christian Mysticism: The Essential Guide to Contemplative Spirituality.* Charlottesville, Va.: Hampton Roads, 2010.

McLaren, Brian. *A Generous Orthodoxy.* Grand Rapids, Mich.: Zondervan, 2004.

——. *A New Kind of Christianity: Ten Questions That Are Transforming the Faith.* New York: HarperCollins, 2010.

Miller, William. *Make Friends with Your Shadow: How to Accept and Use Positively the Negative Side of Your Personality.* Minneapolis, Minn.: Augsburg, 1981.

——. *Your Golden Shadow: Discovering and Fulfilling Your Undeveloped Self.* San Francisco: Harper San Francisco, 1989.

Moore, Robert. *Facing the Dragon: Confronting Personal and Spiritual Grandiosity.* Wilmette, Ill.: Chiron, 2003.

Murphy, Desmond. *A Return to Spirit After the Mythic Church.* New York: Crossroad, 1997.

Naranjo, Claudio. *The Divine Child and the Hero: Inner Meaning in Children's Literature.* Nevada City, Calif.: Gateways, 1999.

Needleman, Jacob. *Time and Soul: Where Has All the Meaningful Time Gone — and Can We Get It Back?* San Francisco: Berrett-Koehler, 2003.

Newberg, Andrew. *Why We Believe What We Believe: Uncovering Our Biological Need for Meaning, Spirituality, and Truth.* New York: Free Press, 2006.

O'Murchu, Diarmuid. *Quantum Theology.* New York: Crossroad, 1997.

Palmer, Parker. *A Hidden Wholeness.* San Francisco: Jossey-Bass, 2004.

Panikkar, Raimon. *A Dwelling Place for Wisdom.* Louisville, Ky.: Westminster/John Knox Press, 1993.

_____. *Christophany: The Fullness of Man.* Maryknoll, N.Y.: Orbis Books, 2004.

Pearce, Joseph Chilton. *Spiritual Initiation and the Breakthrough of Consciousness.* Rochester, Vt.: Park Street Press, 1981.

Pearson, Carol. *The Hero Within: Six Archetypes We Live By.* New York: Harper & Row, 1986.

Plotkin, Bill. *Soulcraft: Crossing into Mysteries of Nature and Psyche.* Novato, CA: New World Library, 2003.

_____. *Nature and the Human Soul: Cultivating Wholeness and Community in a Fragmented World.* Novato, CA: New World Library, 2008.

Smith, Cyprian. *The Way of Paradox.* London: Darton, Longman and Todd, 2004.

Smith, Huston. *Forgotten Truth.* San Francisco: Harper San Francisco, 1976.

St. John of the Cross. *Living Flame of Love.* (E. Peers, ed. and trans.). New York: Triumph Books, 1991.

Stein, Murray. *In Midlife: A Jungian Perspective.* Dallas, Tex.: Spring Publications, 1994.

Tarnas, Richard. *The Passion of the Western Mind: Understanding the Ideas That Have Shaped Our World View.* New York: Ballantine Books, 1991.

Taylor, Charles. *A Secular Age.* Cambridge, Mass.: Belknap Harvard, 2007.

Toolan, David. *At Home in the Cosmos.* Maryknoll, N.Y.: Orbis Books, 2003.

Tracy, David. *Blessed Rage for Order: The New Pluralism in Theology.* New York: Seabury Press, 1979.

Tugwell, Simon. *Ways of Imperfection: An Exploration of Christian Spirituality.* Springfield, Ill.: Templegate, 1985.

Underhill, Evelyn. *The Ways of the Spirit.* New York: Crossroad, 1993.

Watts, Alan. *Behold the Spirit: A Study in the Necessity of Mystical Religion.* New York: Vintage Books, 1972.

Whyte, David. *The Three Marriages: Reimagining Work, Self and Relationship.* New York: Riverhead Books, 2009.

Wilber, Ken. *The Essential Ken Wilber: An Introductory Reader.* Boston: Shambhala, 1998.

———. *The Simple Feeling of Being: Embracing Your True Nature.* Boston: Shambhala, 2004.

———. *Integral Spirituality: A Startling New Role for Religion in the Modern and Postmodern World.* Boston: Shambhala, 2006.

Wilber, Ken, Jack Engler, and Daniel Brown. *Transformations of Consciousness: Conventional and Contemplative Perspectives on Development.* Boston: New Science Library, 1986.

Xavier, N. S. *The Two Faces of Religion: A Psychiatrist's View.* Tuscaloosa, Ala.: Portals, 1987.

Richard Rohr, OFM is a globally recognized ecumenical teacher bearing witness to the universal awakening within Christian mysticism and the Perennial Tradition. He is a Franciscan priest of the New Mexico Province and founder of the Center for Action and Contemplation (CAC www.cac.org) in Albuquerque, New Mexico, where he also serves as the Academic Dean of the Living School for Action and Contemplation. Fr Richard's teaching is grounded in the Franciscan alternative orthodoxy – practices of contemplation and self-emptying, expressing itself in radical compassion, particularly for the socially marginalized. He is the author of numerous books including *The Divine Dance*, *Breathing Under Water* and *Immortal Diamond* (SPCK, 2016, 2016 and 2013 respectively) and the forthcoming *Another Name for Everything*.

A

Abraham (biblical figure),
    8, 21, 23
Adam and Eve, xx, 31, 58–59,
    106
Adolescence, 6, 23, 26–27
Aeneas, 50
Albertz, Rainer, 172n3
Alcoholics Anonymous, 19, 67,
    85, 154
American Idol, heroism and, 20
Amish, as true conservatives, 40
Amnesia: about divinization, 98;
    consequences of, 101; divine
    union and, 100; healing of, 104;
    identity and, 97–98
Anger, 31–32, 123, 133, 135
Animas Institute, 43
Anxiety, 110–115, 134
Apostle's Creed, 50
Archimedes, vii, 27
Art, religious, 117
Art of Loving, The (Fromm), 32
"As Kingfishers Catch Fire"
    (Hopkins), x
Atheism, 174ch9n2
Atonement, 68, 172ch5n1
Augustine, xxi, 113
Authority, xxxiv, 38–39

B

Balance, 28
Barfield, Owen, 37

Beatitudes, 119
Beck, Don, 171n3
Becker, Ernest, xxiv
Belief, versus knowing, 95
Bible, translations used, 169
Blake, William, 103
Bonaventure (saint), 8, 113
Both-and thinking, 146–151
Brothers Karamazov
    (Dostoyevsky), 118
Brueggemann, Walter, 172n3
Buddhism, 59, 68, 148
Butcher, Carmen Adevedo,
    174ch9n2

C

Calling, first and second, 23
Campbell, Joseph, 17
Catholic Church: as accountability
    community, 79–80; as bride,
    80–81; communion and, 103;
    conservatism in, 40; father
    wounds and, 41–43; good old
    days in, 39; institutionalization
    in, 139; liturgy and, 139;
    necessary suffering and, 74–75;
    as paradox, 107–108; scandal
    in, 41; Second Body of Christ
    and, 79; as unified field, 75;
    wisdom of nuns in, 12;
    worldview of, 75–76
Catholic Workers, as true
    conservatives, 40

Cavafy, C. P., 96

Center for Action and
    Contemplation, 124,
    175ch12n1

Change, resistance to, 11–12

Childhood: conditional and
    unconditional love and, 32–33;
    law and limits and, 25–26, 29,
    30, 37

Chodron, Pema, 129

Church, universal: early
    Christianity and, 103; Eastern
    Church fathers and,
    173–174ch8n1; elitism and
    egalitarianism in, 103–104;
    emerging Christianity and, 142,
    145; Jesus' definition of church
    and, 139–140; repeated
    crucifixion of Christ and, 80

Church fathers, on
    divinization, 98

Clare of Assisi, 157

Clement, Olivier, 173–174ch8n1

Clergy, 15, 41–42, 128, 129

Cloud of Unknowing, The
    (Butcher), 174ch9n2

Common good, heroism and, 20

Conscience, internalized, 49

Conservatism, 25, 28, 40, 46

Contemplation, 144, 146, 164,
    171n3

Contentment, 60

Conversion, x, 69–70

Covetousness, 29–30

Criminal justice, 23. *See also* Jails
    and prisons

Culture, xiii–xiv, 6, 27, 82

D

Dalai Lama, xxviii, 80, 137

Dance: cosmic, 122; general, 120,
    122, 167; survival versus sacred,
    xviii, 14, 71–72, 166

Dante, 47

D'Arcy, Paula, 66

David (biblical king), 23

Day, Dorothy, 161

Death: acceptance of, xxxvi;
    avoidance of, 79; denial of, xxiv;
    mystery of, 112; of self, 85; as
    subject in literature, 78–79;
    transition between halves of life
    and, 50–51

Democracy, 9

Depression, 135–136

Dillard, Annie, 53, 59, 90

Dionysius, 113

Disability, 56

Divine Comedy (Dante), 47

Divine gaze, 5–6, 156, 159–160

Divinization, 78, 98, 173ch6n2

Doubt, 110–115

Down-up pattern: faith and trust
    and, xxvi–xxvii; falling upward
    and, xxv–xxvi; in legends and
    literature, xviii–xix; perfection
    and goodness and, xxii–xxiii;
    resistance to, xxiii–xxiv; in

science, xix, xxv; as secret of the soul, xviii, xxvi; in spirituality, xix–xxii; tragic sense of life and, 58–59; trampoline effect and, 158

Dualism: bipartisanship versus transpartisanship and, 171n3; versus both-and thinking, 146–151; creation and evolution and, 93–94; immaturity and, 40; law and freedom and, 36; versus peace, 140; sequencing of, 147; in Thomas Merton's writings, 162

Duns Scotus, John, 57, 169n2

E

Education, grade inflation and, 31

Ego: boundaries and, 147; deconstruction of, xxxiv; economy of merit and, 104; egocentrism and, 11, 43, 65; failure and, 66; foil for, 33–34; limitation of, 28–29, 37; loyal soldier and, 47; pick-and-choose morality and, 27; status-quo preference of, xxiv, xxv; structure of, 4–5, 25, 36, 148, xxiv; superiority complex and, 118; undercutting of, 31; wheel of development and, 171n5

Einstein, Albert, 10, 75, 111

Elders: as "grand" parents, 124; hereness of, 119–120; human fullness of, 153–154; mirroring and, 156; stages of development and, 9

Eliot, T. S., 19, 87, 113

Enlightenment, tradition and, 37

Enneagram, 61, 172n2

Entitlement, sense of, 33

Erikson, Erik, 8, 20, 121

Eros, xiv, 20

Esau (biblical figure), xvi

Esther (biblical queen), 18

Evangelicals, neoconservatism and, 40

Eve (biblical figure). *See* Adam and Eve

F

Failure: balance and, 28; ego and, 66; God's providence and, 56–57; lack of apology and, 58; opportunity and, 158; purpose of, xv; redemption and, 60; wholeness and, 59

Faith, xxvi–xxvii, 63, 100, 111

Family, 22, 82–85

Fear, 6, 11

Field, unified. *See* Unified field

First half of life: big three concerns of, 4; calling and, 23; churches' validation of, xvii; creation of container and, xiii, 1, 13, 27–28; done poorly, 38–43;

dualistic thinking and, 36; as
    foundation of house, xvii–xviii;
    Gospel in, 139; identity and,
    4–6; infantile grandiosity and,
    71; institutions in, 141; lessons
    of, 45–46; loyal soldier and,
    45–46, 47; mirroring and, 157;
    naiveté of, 112–113; provisional
    personality in, 147; purity and,
    xxiii; regressive restoration of,
    40, 41–43; security and, 6; Ten
    Commandments and, 119; as
    warm-up act, viii; wisdom in,
    139; writing the text and, 143.
    See also Life transition
Forgiveness, 57, 102–103, 148
Four Quartets (Eliot), 113
Fowler, James, 8
Francis of Assisi: conditional and
    unconditional love and, 32;
    journey of, 18, 23; on kissing a
    leper, 69–70; lifetime of falling
    and, 124–125; spirituality of
    imperfection and, xxiv
Franciscans: as accountability
    community, 79–80; as bride,
    81; God and humanity and,
    172ch5n1; particular stories
    and, 57; Rohr as, 74; rules
    and, 39
Frank, Anne, 10
Frankl, Victor, 114
Freedom: forgiveness and,
    102–103; inner, 87, 118; law
    and, 35–36; love and, 79; to say
    yes or no, 79; self-exclusion

and, 102; in Thomas Merton's
    writings, 162–163, 166; truth
    and, 74
Freud, Sigmund, 47, 60
Friendship, mirroring and, 156
Fromm, Eric, 32, 33
Frost, Robert, 4
Fundamentalism, xxxi,
    174ch9n2

G

Gandhi, 10, 12
Gebser, Jean, 8
Generativity, 20, 154
Gethsemani monastery, 161
Gilligan, Carol, 8
Girard, Rene, 29
Globalization, identity politics
    and, 40
God: authentic experience of, 13;
    children of, 2; compassion of,
    56–57; conspiracy of, 92;
    creation and, 65, 93; desire and,
    89, 94–95; disappointment in,
    165–166; as Driver, 167; failure
    and success and, 158; falling
    into, 125; filling of vacuums
    and, 160; free will and, 79; gaze
    of, 5; goodness of, 80, 111;
    hiddenness in, 130; inner
    experience of, 122; kingdom of,
    xxxvi; love of, 33; mercy of,
    58–59; mind of humanity and,
    172ch5n1; as mysterious and
    outpouring, 121; obedience
    to, 22; parts and the Whole

and, xxxiv; paths toward and away from, 60–61; perfect receiving and, 159–160; presence of, 63; qualities of, 109–110; as stumbling stone, 65; superego and, 47–48; Ten Commandments and, xxviii; transformation and, 50–51; True Self and, ix–xi, 86, 90–91; union with, 12; vision of, 166; voice of, 46–47, 48, 84

Goodness, xxii–xxiii, 80, 122,

Gospel: big message of, 76; creation and, 77; in first half of life, 139; as good news, 71, 98; healing and growth and, 59; leaving home and, 38; problem inside a solution and, 159; spiritual journey and, 138; tragic sense of life and, 58; as wedding partner, 81

Grace: versus certainty, 56; economy of, 104; life transition and, xvi–xvii; redemption and, 60; stumbling and, 65

Graves, Clare, 8, 171n3

Gregory of Nyssa, 51, 97

H

Hades, Odysseus in, xxxiv

Hafiz, 13

Halves of life: metaphors for, 2; as morning and afternoon, 1; necessity of, 2–3; no versus yes and, 142; old and new wineskins and, 2; outer and

inner journey and, xxxiv–xxxv; Rohr's reasons for writing about, vii–viii, xiv–xvi; tablets of the law and, xxviii; vocabularies of, xxvii. *See also* First half of life; Life transition; Second half of life

Happiness, meaning and, 113–114

Heaven: as charged concept, ix; divine union and, 100; exclusion versus inclusion and, 101–102; hell and, 49–50; life's journey and, xi–xii; now and later, 95–96, 100–102; practicing for, 101; as state of consciousness, 104

Hell: as charged concept, ix; heaven and, 49–50; life's journey and, xi–xii; loss of divine union and, 100; in the present, 101; self-exclusion and, 102; as state of consciousness, 104

Heraclites, 78

Hercules, 50

Hermes, 50

Heroes and heroines, 17, 18–24

Hesse, Hermann, 90

Hinduism, 5, 103

Holiness, 48, 132, 135

Hollis, James, 25

Holocaust, 113, 130

Holy Spirit, 88, 90, 91–92, 111

Home: being versus doing and, 94; as goal of sacred story, 87–91

Homer, xxxii–xxxiii, xxxvi,
    87, 88
Hope, Holy Spirit and, 92
Hopkins, Gerard Manley, x, 78,
    124, 169n2
Hospice, 130, 158
Hubris, 58, 71
Humiliation: Rohr's prayer for,
    128; self-knowledge and,
    130–131; shadow work and,
    164; stumbling and, 66; tragic
    sense of life and, 63
Humility, holiness and, 132
Hypocrisy, 132

I

Identity: versus commonality, 120;
    divine gaze and, 5–6; Japanese
    soldiers and, 43–44; mistaken,
    97–98; narcissistic fix and, 4–6;
    persona and shadow self and,
    127–129, 131–132, 133; as
    place to stand, 27; religion and,
    12–13; True Self and, 86
Indigenous people, healthy
    psyches of, 36–37
Initiation. *See* Male initiation
Institutions, 137–142. *See also*
    specific institutions
Integral Theory, 171n3
Integrity, xv
Irenaeus, 97
Iroquois Nation, 32
Isaiah (prophet), 49, 65, 151
Islam, 13, 103, 118

"Ithaca" (Cavafy), 96
I-Thou relationships, 159

J

Jacob (biblical figure), xvi, xix
Jails and prisons, 23, 34,
    40–41, 70
Japan, 43–44
Jaspers, Karl, 30, 80
Jefferson, Thomas, 9
Jeremiah (prophet), 49
Jesus: as alpha and omega, 89; on
    befriending opponents, 129; on
    binding and loosing, 142;
    both-and thinking of, 148,
    149–150; calling of disciples by,
    22–23; on change, 11; church
    practice and, 56; as Cosmic
    Christ, 169invitation n2,
    172ch5n1; criticism of own
    religion by, 10; crucifixion of,
    xxiv, 68–69, 80, 166, 172ch5n1;
    definition of church and,
    139–140; on doing God's will,
    34–35; down-up pattern and,
    xviii, xx–xxi; family and, 22, 82,
    83, 84; on first and last, xxiii;
    foolish-sounding wisdom
    of, 12; on gaining the world, 72;
    on God's gifts, 109; on good
    trees and bad, xiv; on goodness
    of God, 80; healing stories
    and, 61, 102–103; heaven and
    hell and, 50, 101; incarnation
    and, 57; John the Baptist and, 5;

journeys and, 44; on kingdom of God, 100, 101; on lamp of the body, 157; on lamp within, 128, 130; on law and freedom, 35–36; on least of these, 55; on life beyond security, 7; on living water, 67–68, 154; on losing our life, 85; lost-and-found parables of, 67; on obedience, 22; on old and new wineskins, 2; outsiders and, 56; on pearls before swine, 11–12; on Pharisee and tax collector, 45; on plank in eye, 130; process language and, 8; on prodigal son, 45; redemption and, 34; as risen Christ, 58; Samaritan woman and, 96; as savior, 108; on sowing seeds, 142; as spiritual authority, 81; on straining out gnats, 47–48; as teacher who said yes, 142–143; tragic sense of life and, 53, 59; transfiguration and, xxvii; on unclean spirit, 62; on wisdom, xxi–xxii; wounds of, 19

Jews and Judaism, 101, 103, 111, 172n3

Joan of Arc, 18

John of the Cross, 8, 50–51, 117, 166

John of the Ladder, 8

John Paul II (pope), 104

John the Baptist, 5

John XXIII (pope), 13

Journeys, xi–xii, xxxii–xxxvii, 18–24, 44

Julian of Norwich, xx, 58, 103, 136

Jung, Carl: on goals, xiii; on morning and afternoon of life, 1; on mysteries of life, 88; on stumbling, 58; on suffering, 73; on two halves of life, 8

K

Kabir, 13

Kegan, Robert, 171n3

Keller, Helen, 154

Keyes, Kin, 7–8

King, Martin Luther, Jr., 10, 12

Kohlberg, Lawrence, 8, 171n3

Kohut, Heinz, 157

L

Law and limits: broken tablets and, xxviii; Franciscans and, 39; freedom and, 35–36; as goad to kick against, 33, 46; healthy growth and, 25–26, 28–29, 34; immature responses to, 36; institutions and, 137–138; legalism and, 40–41; misuse of, 38; predictability and, 29–30; presumption against, 37; proving of purpose of, 39

Liberation, 8, 39

Life transition: as adventure, xvii; crossover points and, viii–ix; from elitism to egalitarianism

and, 103; falling upward and,
xxvi; grace and, xvi–xvii,
23–24; inhibition of, 160; loyal
soldier and, 43–44; luck and,
165; mystery and, 49–51; pain
and, 160; sequencing and, xv;
simplicity and, 114–115;
wisdom and, 138
Liminal space, 50, 171–172n7
Loneliness, 143–145
Love: civilization of, 32; falling in,
xxvi–xxvii; freedom and, 79;
great, 61; possession and, 124;
as subject in literature, 78;
unconditional and conditional,
32–33
Lucifer, 133

M

Magdalene (biblical figure), 23
Male initiation: childhood toys in,
xxxv; heroic journey and, 18;
"life is hard" message in,
73–74; liminal space and,
171–172n7; M.A.L.E. and,
175ch11n1; side-to-side
movement and, xxv; wheel of
development and, 171n5
Mandela, Nelson, 10, 12
Mary (mother of Jesus), 92
Maslow, Abraham, 6, 8, 171n3
Maturation: acceptance of reality
and, 7; both-and thinking
and, 10; boundaries and, 10;
charting movement and
direction and, 8–9; family

and, 83; grace and, xvi–xvii;
growth in seeing and, 130;
liberation and, 39; mirroring
and, 157–158; peacefulness
and, 133; religion and, 99–100;
resistance to change and,
11–12; second simplicity and,
108; steps and stages of, 8–12;
stretching and, 10–11, 12;
structure and authority and, 38;
transcending and including
and, xxvii–xxviii, 9–10, 35;
transpartisanship versus
bipartisanship and, 40
McLaren, Brian, 101
Meaning, happiness and, 113–114
Mennonites, as true
conservatives, 40
Meritocracy, 45
Merton, Thomas: on brightness,
115; on cosmic dance, 122;
influence of, 161–162;
influences on, 169n2; on ladder
of success, xvii; on personal
salvation projects, 21; as Rohr's
teacher, 161; on self, 173ch6n2;
"When in the Soul of the
Serene Disciple" (Merton) and,
162–167
Milan, Cesar, 29
Mirroring: admiration and
criticism and, 155; divine, 5–6,
158; divine gaze and, 159–160;
I-Thou relationships and, 159;
maturation and, 157–158; real
self and, 155–157; reflecting

what we fight and, 118; service and, 154; spiritual gifts and, 157

Mohammed, 8

Montessori, Maria, 29

Moore, Robert, 71

Morality, superego and, 47–48

Mormons, 40

Moses, xxviii, 8, 82

Mother Teresa, 10, 80, 111

Muir, John, 32

Mystery: Catholic Church and, 76; conspiracy of God and, 92; doubt and, 111–112; engagement with, 98; grace as, xviii; life as pause between, 88; myth and, xxx; paschal, xxi; of self, x; stumbling and, 65; transition between halves of life and, 51; wisdom and, 112

Mysticism: Catholic Church and, 76; incarnational, 78–79; reading in second half of life and, 144; science and, 157; spiritual journey and, 103

Myths, xxix–xxxi, 92–93,

N

Name of the Rose, The (Eco), 118

Narcissism: authority and, 34; extended adolescence and, 26–27; narcissistic fix and, 4–6; in old age, 3; politeness and, 11

Native Americans, sweat lodge and, 103

Nativity, birth of God in the soul and, 14

Nature. *See* Science and nature

Nazis, 130

Neighbors, fences and, 4

Neurosis, as norm, 37

Newton, Isaac, 54–59

Nicholas of Cusa, 113

Nuremburg trials, 130

O

Obedience, 22, 26

Odysseus: heroic journeys and, xxxii–xxxvi, 18, 19, 22, 23; home and, 88, 89–90, 94, 96; losses of, 67, 69; as loyal soldier, 47; myth and, xxxi–xxxii; realm of death and, 50; shadow side of, 131; Teiresias's prophecy and, xxxiii–xxxvi; tragedy and, 58

Odyssey, The (Homer). *See* Odysseus

Oliver, Mary, 1

Orpheus, 50

Orthodox Church, 117, 139

P

Palmer, Parker, 80

Parenting, 30

Particular, scandal of, 57

Pastoral ministry, 15

Paul (apostle): on angels of darkness, 133; on being hidden in God, 130; on Damascus Road, 67; on discerning of spirits, xiv; holy foolishness and, 134; on Jesus as teacher,

142–143; journey of, 23; on law, 34, 35–36; on least of these, 55; spirituality of imperfection and, xxiv; on wisdom, 151

Peace, versus dualistic bickering, 140

Peace Corps, 22

Pearl of great price, 86

Pearls before swine, 11–12

Peck, Scott, xix

Perfection and imperfection: contentment and, 60; falling upward and, xxvi; goodness and, xxii–xxiii; imposition of order and, 62; in natural world, 55–56; spirituality of, xxiv

Piaget, Jean, 8, 171n3

Plato: church practice and, 56; on democracy, 9; perfect forms and, 55; tragic gaps and, 80; world of ideas and, 130

Plotkin, Bill: on patho-adolescence, 27; process language and, 8; on survival dance, xviii; vision quests and, 43; wheel of development and, 171n5

Poetry, 144

Politics, 31–32, 40, 118–119

Poor Clares, 40

Postmodernism, 93

Prayer: deep time and, xxx; divine gaze and, 5; for humiliation, 128; versus knee-jerk responses, 118–119; life as, xxix

Preaching, 7, 14

Prisons and jails. *See* Jails and prisons

Process language, 8

Prodigal son, 45

Prophets, 12, 53

Providence, 56–57

Q

Quakers, as true conservatives, 40

R

Rationality, religion and, 105

Reality: eternal, 95–96; mirroring and, 155–156

Reformation, 37

Religion: againstness and, 142; Big Picture and, 109; boundaries and, 10; coherent universe and, 111; criticism of, 74; diversity and, 60; early-stage, 13–14, 45; as evacuation plan, 101; founding myths of, 21–22; functions of, 170ch1n2; fundamentalism in, xxxi, 38; identity and, 12–13; leaving family and, 84–85; mature, 99–100; means and goals and, xxviii–xxix; myth and, xxxi; neoconservatism in, 40; new tribalism in, 39–40; participation and, xi; parts and the Whole and, xxxiv–xxxv; rationality and, 105; reality and, 95; resistance to change and, 11; science and, 93–94; security and, 6–7; True Self and, 98; unified field and, 59

Repentance, x

Ricoeur, Paul, 105, 108

Rilke, Rainer Maria, 26, 153

Ritual, 44

Ritual Process, The (Turner), 171–172n7

Road Less Traveled, The (Peck), xix

Rohr, Richard, life journey of, 105–110

Roosevelt, Eleanor, 32

Roots of Christian Mysticism, The (Clement), 173–174ch8n1

Rumi, 13

S

Sacrifice, xxxv, 26

Sadness, 117, 122, 135–136

Salvation: narcissistic fix and, 5–6; order as, 38–39; personal project of, 21; sin and, 60–61; thinking and, 56; tragic sense of life and, 59

Sarah (biblical figure), 8, 21

Science and nature: down-up pattern in, xix, xxv; First Body of Christ and, 79; groaning of creation and, 77–82; mysticism and, 157; religion and, 93–94; tragic natural world and, 54–59; unified field and, 78, 79; universality and, 57; wonderful and terrible in, 78

Second half of life: Beatitudes and, 119; being and doing and, 123; calling and, 23; chronology and, xvi; commentary on the text and, 143; contents of container and, xiii, 1, 121; discerning of spirits and, xiv; double belonging and, 145; family and community of origin and, 83–84; friendship in, 137; general dance and, 120–121; generativity in, 121; generosity in, 124; hereness and, 119–120; as higher stage, 3; inner freedom and, 87; inner restlessness and, 94–95; institutions in, 137–139, 140–141; lightness in, 117; loyal soldier and, 47, 48–49; mirroring in, 156; opinions and, 122–123; paradox and, 114; politics and, 118–119; prayer and, xxix; religious substance and, 13; as second childhood, 104; second simplicity and, 108; self-criticism and, 130–131; service in, 154; solitude in, 143–144; tools for, xxxv; voice of God in, 48; withdrawal from evil things and, 118. *See also* Life transition

Security, 6–8

Self: false, 85–86, 99, 101, 132; hatred of, 132; justification of, 129; knowledge of, 134; mirroring and, 155–157;

self-criticism and, 130–131;
   self-image and, 31, 118,
   128–130; strong, 26; Thomas
   Merton on, 173ch6n2. *See also*
   Shadow work; True Self
Selfishness, 26
Seminary education, 41–42
Seton, Elizabeth, 121
Seven Storey Mountain (Merton),
   162
Shadow work: criticism and, 155;
   depression and sadness and,
   135–136; holiness and sin and,
   132–133; humiliation and, 131,
   164; persona and shadow self
   and, 127–129, 131–132,
   133–134; seeing the shadow
   and, 134; self-image and,
   129–130
Shakers, as true conservatives, 40
Siddhartha, 18
Sign of Jonah (Merton), 161
Simplicity, 108, 114–115, 120, 121
Sin: down-up pattern and, xx–xxi;
   gifts and, 61, 172n2; Jesus and,
   59; redemption and, 60;
   salvation and, 60–61; versus
   shadow, 132–133; superficiality
   and, 95; transformation and,
   61–62
Slavery, 71–72
Soldier, loyal, 44, 45–50, 83
Solitude, 143–145, 164
Soul: birth of God in, 14; finding
   of, 19; as God-given, ix; home
   and, xxxvii; inner abiding

and, 91; as inner blueprint, ix,
   xi; soul centric worldview
   and, 43; soul encounter and,
   171n5; stewardship of, ix–x
Spiral Dynamics, 8, 171n3
Spiritual direction, 14, 50, 172n2
Spiritual gifts, 157
Spirituality: conspiracy of God
   and, 92; as imitation of God,
   103; superficial expressions
   of, 13; unlearning and, 99–100
Steiner, Rudolf, 29
Steppenwolf (Hesse), 90
Suffering, necessary: Catholic
   Church and, 74–75;
   communion in, 158–159;
   complexity and, 115; false self
   and, 85–86; family and, 82–85;
   groaning of creation and,
   77–82; holy sadness and, 135;
   lack of theology for, 68; as
   legitimate, 73–74; luck and,
   165; stumbling and, ix, 65–67;
   tragic sense of life and, 63
Sullivan, Anne, 154
Superego, 47–48

T

Tea Party movement, 32
Teilhard de Chardin, Pierre, 79,
   109
Ten Commandments, 29–30, 82,
   119
Teresa of Avila, 8, 91, 107, 134
Testament (Francis of Assisi),
   69–70

Thanatos, xiv, 20

"That Nature Is a Heraclitean
    Fire . . ." (Hopkins), 78

Theosis. See Divinization

Therese of Lixieux, xxiv

Thisness, 57, 169n2

Thomas (apostle), 111

Tower of Babel, 30

Tradition: in first half of life, 46;
    healthy growth and, 28–29;
    misuse of, 38; new religious
    tribalism and, 39–40;
    presumption against, 37

Tragic sense of life: in Bible,
    58–59, 62–63; church practice
    and, 80; down-up pattern and,
    58–59; meaning of *tragedy* and,
    58; natural world and, 54–59;
    origin of phrase, 53–54;
    salvation and, 59; solitude and,
    143; transformation and,
    60–63; Western society and, 71

True Self: authentic God
    experience and, 13;
    capitalization of, 169invitation
    n1; deep time and, 101;
    discovery of, 98; false self and,
    85–86; as God-given, ix; heaven
    and, 100–101; home and,
    90–91; versus imitation, 163;
    offense and, 8; search for, 94;
    time and, xi. *See also* Self

Trust, faith and, xxvi–xxvii, 63

Truth: in Bible, 62–63; Big Picture
    and, 109; Enneagram and, 61;
    freedom and, 74; knowledge of,
    98–99; myths and, xxix–xxxi;
    perception of, ix; in praise and
    criticism, 156

Tubman, Harriet, 12

Turner, Victor, 171–172n7

Tutu, Desmond, ix

U

Unamuno, Miguel de, 53–54

Unified field: Albert Einstein and,
    111; compassion and, 59;
    first-stage survival and, xviii;
    Holy Spirit and, 90; inclusion
    and, 114; knowledge and, 99;
    necessary suffering and, 75,
    78–79; "up" and, 151

United States, as paradox,
    107–108

V

Values, internalization of, 26

W

War, 62

Western society: amnesia of, 98;
    dualism in, 36; identity in, 27;
    Jesus' authority in, 81; myths
    and, xxix–xxx; neuroses in, 37;
    as ritually starved, 44; tragic
    sense of life and, 71

"When in the Soul of the Serene
    Disciple" (Merton), 162–167

Wholeness, 48, 151

Wilber, Ken: on calling beliefs
    into question, 12; on classic
    spiritual journey, 103; on

functions of religion, 170ch1n2; Integral Theory and, 171n3; process language and, 8; on rationality, 105
Wineskins, old and new, 2
Winfrey, Oprah, 34
Wisdom: in first half of life, 139; versus knowledge, 151; life transition and, 138; mystery and, 112; *Odyssey, The* (Homer) and, xxxvi
Wizard of Oz, 90
Women religious, 12

Wordsworth, William, 99
Workplace, 33
Woundedness: father wounds and, 41; healing and growth and, 35; imperfection and, xxiv; resistance to change and, 67; victimhood and, 34

Y

Yeats, William Butler, 15

Z

Zen, 86, 130